NINE UNIVERSITY PRESIDENTS WHO SAVED THEIR INSTITUTIONS

The Difference in Effective Administration

NINE UNIVERSITY PRESIDENTS WHO SAVED THEIR INSTITUTIONS
The Difference in Effective Administration

Edward J. Kormondy
and
Kent M. Keith

With a Preface by
E. K. Fretwell

The Edwin Mellen Press
Lewiston•Queenston•Lampeter

Library of Congress Cataloging-in-Publication Data

Kormondy, Edward John, 1926-
Nine university presidents who saved their institutions : the difference in effective
administration / Edward J. Kormondy and Kent M. Keith ; with a preface by E. K. Fretwell.
p. cm.
Includes bibliographical references and index.
ISBN-13: 978-0-7734-5164-3
ISBN-10: 0-7734-5164-1
1. Universities and colleges--United States--Presidents--Biography. 2. Universities and
colleges--United States--Administration. 3. Leadership. I. Keith, Kent M. II. Title.
LB2341.K67 2008
378.1'11--dc22
[B]
                                                                    2008004945
hors série.

A CIP catalog record for this book is available from the British Library.

Front cover: Tusculum College Arch

The Edwin Mellen Press   The Edwin Mellen Press
Box 450   Box 67
Lewiston, New York   Queenston, Ontario
USA 14092-0450   CANADA L0S 1L0

The Edwin Mellen Press, Ltd.
Lampeter, Ceredigion, Wales
UNITED KINGDOM SA48 8LT

Printed in the United States of America

Dedication

This book is dedicated to past, present, and future
college and university presidents who have saved or will
save their institutions from having to close their doors
and to boards of trustees who are seeking such presidents.

Table of Contents

PREFACE

This is a remarkable piece of work! It presents a series of nine case studies of higher education institutions that were salvaged from what appeared to be failures—sudden but more typically gradual. In each case, the salvaging president or chancellor (the "hero/heroine") was the critical factor who identified and traveled the road to success. The turnaround ranged from one or two years to as many as eight years.

Beyond the campus leader acting in these dramatic situations were faculty, alumni, students, staff, towns people and, indeed, trustees. But, in a shockingly large number of cases, trustees were not alert to the crisis until red signals were flashing. In more than one case, presidents required a great deal of spine to disagree with a board chairman on a major issue, even putting their jobs on the line.

For whom can this study be of particular value?

1. Trustees, many of whom were a major part of the solutions, their attention was focused, and they teamed with their presidents.

2. Presidents themselves, including those not yet in trouble who could spot danger points and (hopefully) avoid them.

3. Faculty members who need to know that the institution can be saved and who must provide focus on the intellectual and professional aspects of the institution.

4. Accrediting agencies who shared their powers to suggest steps toward recovery and, where necessary, to carry and use a big stick.

5. Citizens, (including bankers who were sometimes willing to take a significant risk) who realized the importance of a healthy institution in their communities.

6. Others, including alumni, who can choose to sit silently by or become generous supporters.

* * * * * *

Concerning presidents, while those interviewed said they would "do it again," they deserve commendation for dangerous duty. Some of them, including members of their families faced unusual stresses, including the possibility of physical harm. (One found a bullet hole in his office window and used an armed guard to take his three-year-old to kindergarten.)

The authenticity of conclusions and findings is due to Edward Kormondy and Kent Keith. "They've been there."

E. K. Fretwell

E. K. Fretwell is Chancellor Emeritus of the University of North Carolina at Charlotte where he served ten years as chancellor. Following retirement in 1989, he was interim president of the five-campus University of Massachusetts system. Earlier, he was president of State University of New York, College at Buffalo. His study on interim presidents, The Interim Presidency: Guidelines for University and College Governing Boards, was published by the Association of Governing Boards. With David Leslie as senior author, he wrote Wise Moves in Hard Times. Active in national organizations, he has served as elected head of the American Association of State Colleges and Universities, The American Council on Education, and the Carnegie Foundation for the Advancement of Teaching, among others.

Acknowledgments

We gratefully acknowledge those who helped us identify the presidents who turned around their institutions for this study. Our thanks go to Dr. Charles M. Cook, then Director, Commission on Institutions of Higher Education, New England Association of Schools and Colleges; Dr. Steven D. Crow, Executive Director, Commission on Institutions of Higher Education, North Central Association of Colleges and Schools; Dr. James T. Rogers, then Executive Director, Commission on Colleges, Southern Association of Colleges and Schools; Dr. David B. Wolf, then Executive Director, Accrediting Commission of Community and Junior Colleges, Western Association of Schools and Colleges; and Mr. Ralph A. Wolff, Executive Director, Accrediting Commission for Senior Colleges and Universities, Western Association of Schools and Colleges.

We are most grateful to the thirty-six presidents who completed the survey instrument and the ten presidents who made themselves available for individual interviews; unfortunately, one of these ten presidents withdrew her interview on advice of her board chair. This was another East Coast Baccalaureate institution.

Included in the survey was the option of retaining confidentiality of both or either the institution and the individual; twenty-two of the respondents permitted release of their name and nineteen of their institution's name as follows: Dr. Donald F. Averill, Palo Verde College; Dr. Michael S. Bassis, Olivet College; Dr. Laurence M. Conner; Dr. Richard H. Cox; Dr. Thomas E. deWitt, Lasell College; Dr. Alan E. Guskin, Antioch University; Dr. Garry D. Hays, United States International University; Dr. Francis E. Hazard, Urbana University; Mr. Neil J. Hoffman, Otis College of Art and Design; Dr. Kent M. Keith, Chaminade University of Honolulu; Dr. Robert E. Knott, Tusculum College; Dr. Edward J. Kormondy, University of West Los Angeles; Mr. Paul J. LeBlanc; Dr. Jerry C. Lee, National University; Dr. Steven C. Morgan, University of La Verne; Mr. Daniel L. Ritchie, University of Denver; Dr.

Thomas M. Stauffer, Golden Gate University; Dr. Peggy A Stock, Colby-Sawyer College; Dr. Haywood L. Strickland; Dr. James Waddell, Menlo College; Mr. Chatt G. Wright, Hawai'i Pacific University; and Dr. Richard E. Wylie, Endicott College. To all these individuals and the fourteen presidents who preferred confidentiality, we are deeply indebted and express our appreciation for their participation.

Helen Rogers, Reference Librarian at the University of Hawai'i-Hilo, used her wizardry in locating missing components of some of the references. Thank you, Helen.

Edward J. Kormondy
Chancellor Emeritus, University of Hawai'i-Hilo
Former President, University of West Los Angeles

Kent M. Keith
Chief Executive Officer, The Greenleaf Center for Servant-Leadership
Former President, Chaminade University of Honolulu

Introduction

Background

Although colleges and universities are established with the best of intentions to last into the indefinite future, hundreds have failed and gone out of business or merged with other institutions. Rudolph (1962) estimated that more than 700 colleges died in the United States before 1860, and more than 170 private colleges closed their doors between 1965 and 1986 (Sellars 1994). Rhodes (2006) posited that 583 colleges and universities, 48 public and 535 private, closed between 1966 and 2006. while 900 four-year and 900 two-year colleges were established in the same period. More explicitly, during the seven year period from AY 2000 through 2006, eighty-nine higher education institutions closed, and sixty underwent mergers (Rodenhouse 2001, 2002; Burke, 2003, 2004, 2005, 2006, 2007). Joining these obituaries in 2008 is distinguished Antioch College (Fain 2007, Carlson 2007, Keyes 2007), which is profiled below. Each of these institutions had a president or chancellor, as well as a governing board, who, for whatever reason, were unable to prevent the institution from closing or merging. Think of the displacement of loyal employees, loss of alumnae/alumni identity, and the absence of a cohesive community economic and social engine.

While certain historical periods may have been especially hard on colleges, it is not at all unusual today to find among today's some 4,250 U.S. colleges and universities a number that are in dire straits, faced with closure or a merger, or bogged down in problems that stymie growth and excellence. Standard and Poor's report, "Weak Equity Market Hurt U. S. Education Endowments," predicted that colleges and universities might "...consolidate in large numbers or close as they struggle against stagnant levels of financial resources and substantially higher levels of debt." (van der Werf 2002, A34)

As we will see in what follows, there are some presidents who have succeeded in saving their institutions or launching them in new, more positive directions. Who are these leaders? What issues did they face? What are their backgrounds? How did they accomplish the turn-around and/or put the institution back on the right or a new path?

As most college and university presidents already know, there is a considerable literature on their multi-faceted role (*e.g.*, Kerr (1963,1983), Kerr and Gade (1986), Tierney (1988), Neumann and Bensimon (1990), and Murphy (1997), among others). The Spring/Summer 1996 issue of *The Educational Record* carried several articles that captured a great deal of the ups and downs of the presidency, and the popular literature abounds in self-help approaches to effective leadership in both public and non-profit sectors (*e.g.*, Heifitz (1994); Powell (1995); Zander (1993). Finally, there is always Machiavelli's The Prince. However, there is no current, systematic study of presidents who take on institutions that are *in extremis* in varying degrees and turn them around or at least begin the process of turning them around or even leading them in new directions.

This gap in the literature is important because "turnarounds" reveal both the leadership qualities of a president and the nature of change within academic institutions. There is a crisis; the future of the institution is at stake; decisions have to be made. Presidents have to lead a process of change, under tremendous pressure, with short deadlines. It cannot be business as usual, because business as usual led to the crisis. Issues and alternatives have to be faced, and choices have to be made.

The Salvaging President

For want of a better describer, presidents who lead a turnaround might be described as "salvaging presidents." We (Appendix B) embarked on a project to study such presidents because their insights could teach us about leadership under pressure and the fundamental conditions that must be in place for change to occur on a campus. We also embarked on the study in hopes of providing information and advice that will benefit other presidents in the future. Colleges and universities will continue to face crises in the coming years. It is our hope that this study will help presidents, boards, faculty, and staff understand how to face those crises with intelligence and courage so that their institutions will not only be salvaged but renewed.

The Research Protocol

In addition to our own sphere of colleagues who had been salvagers, we enlisted the support of the regional accrediting associations in a confidential identification of such individuals in their regions. All of the regional accrediting associations except the Middle States Association of Colleges and Schools and the Northwest Association of Schools and Colleges agreed to participate.

Forty nine presidents and former presidents (plus the two of us) were invited to participate in the project, which involved the completion of a five page, largely check-off, survey instrument (Appendix B). The survey consisted of five major sections: the situation at the institution, reason(s) for being appointed, short-term actions and long-term strategies, the turn around, and advice for future "salvagers." Of the fifty-one survey instruments mailed, thirty-six were completed, an excellent response level.

According to the then extant Carnegie Classification, the thirty-six institutions included: four Associate of Arts; two Baccalaureate I; eleven Baccalaureate II; five Masters I; four Masters II; two Doctoral I; two Doctoral II; and six others (two art, two business, one law, one psychology). Twenty-eight of the institutions were independent/non profit, four were public (state and/or local), and four were church affiliated. Geographically, the Northeast region was represented by eight institutions, the Southeast by two, the Midwest by eleven, the Northwest by one, and the Southwest by fourteen. Five of the institutions enrolled fewer than 499 students, nineteen between 500 and 999, six from 1,000 to 1,499, and the remainder scattered to the 9,000 level, with one over 11,000.

Analysis of responses by type (*i.e.*, Carnegie Classification) and size of institution, from fewer than 500 to more than 11,000, demonstrated no distinct patterns or clusters. That is, the issues and their resolution did not vary by the kind or size of institution.

We begin in Part One with a review of the pertinent literature on presidential leadership particularly in struggling institutions and ask the question: Do some presidents make a difference? This sets the stage for the in-depth interviews of nine presidents in Part Two. In Part Three, we provide an analysis of the interviews and, in Part Four, an overview and analysis of the survey results. Part Five covers the lessons learned in the study. The survey instrument and results appear in the Appendix A.

The Characteristics of Struggling Institutions

During the interview with then President of Otis College of Art and Design in Los Angeles and Westchester, CA, Neil Hoffman detailed his observations on the characteristics of struggling institutions. Because his insights are so informative to the centrality of our research, they are presented at length herewith as a direct quote:

> The characteristics of struggling institutions, from my observations, are all the same. First, there is a lack of vision and mission. Usually when the struggling peaks, there is a tendency for people in the institution to say that is the way it has always been. They look to the past for the future, and they hang onto buzz words or phrases as if they are Holy Grail. They are not examined nor critically reviewed. Or, if enrollments are waning and finances are strained, they will change the mission to fit a perceived notion of what will draw students. Either way, you are not defining, extrapolating, and following a vision for the institution.
>
> The second component is leadership. Usually and all too often, there are ill-

defined roles and responsibilities, especially when an institution is struggling. Administrative and academic governance are non-existent or confused. Panic is the everyday event. Where there is some sense of roles and responsibilities, it tends to be based on collective bargaining, a union relationship in a protectionist mode rather than forward-looking. If the Board, administration, faculty, and students do not have clear roles and responsibilities - and, in my experience it is usually all four - you are headed for trouble.

The third component that follows very naturally is that there is a lack of planning. There is a brush fire approach to problem solving. Now, how can you plan if you don't know where you are going? The joke about that is that you redouble your efforts when you have lost sight of the goal. Without a sense of vision, you cannot have a plan.

The next characteristic is enrollment management. If you don't know where you are going, don't have a road map to get you there, and if you are not sure who is on first and what's on second, it affects the recruiting efforts. Catalogs will tend to either stick to what it was that everyone believes the institution has been or wishes to be, and the students will get a confused message from admissions counselors. Admissions work is often regarded as the work of five people in an office instead of management of enrollment throughout the entire institution. There is a dysfunctional fit between what the admissions office is doing and what the faculty or alumni are saying. There is no regular review of admissions information and data; folklore becomes the information base. Myth abounds. Anecdote defines who we are and where we are going rather than real information. So, therefore there is a direct correlation between the vision, how you sell the institution, and attrition rates.

This results in unstable enrollments and the inability to predict enrollments. Since most colleges are tuition-dependent, the financial core of the institution is in jeopardy. Inevitably, there is a financial problem, the fifth characteristic. It could happen for one year, or as is often the case, over the course of several years. If there is any quasi-endowment at all, there is a tendency to throw money at the problem rather than towards a solution. When there is a financial problem, usually the last to know is the Board of Trustees because they are shielded by a veil of ignorance.

All this adds up to a notion that "We are in financial trouble, and we have to get a business person to solve this problem." Now mind you, the problem is not a financial one, that is the outcome. I repeat - no vision, no plan, no leadership. Instead there is a call to go out and raise money. But what are you going to sell if you are not clear about your mission? Further, this is compounded by the mistaken notion that the Vice President for Development raises money. The Vice President for Development does not raise money; he or she makes it happen by 1) a plan that has priorities, and 2) having everyone in the institution have a sense of what their role is.

The final result and characteristic is the negative impact on institutional climate. The most prevailing, difficult problem is that rumors abound - Have you heard the latest? It first starts inside, and then it goes to the community. The place is in trouble. It isn't even based on fact - it's in the water, the dinner party, the cocktail parties.

So of these six things that start with vision and end with climate, the most important are vision and climate. The rest is just management - they are the easiest to quantify and the first to resolve - and a good manager can take care of those things. But vision and climate require leadership. And I believe very strongly that ultimately the most important element is institutional climate.

In summary, the six characteristics developed by Neil Hoffman are: lack of vision and mission, leadership, planning, and enrollment management; unstable enrollments leading to financial stress; and institutional climate (low morale).

As will be evident in the case studies that appear in Part Two and the analysis of them in Part Three, as well as the summary of the survey responses in Part Four, virtually all of the struggling institutions in our study demonstrated all or nearly all of these six characteristics. That in itself is a very compelling lesson for would-be presidents - as well as presidential search consultants, search committees, and boards of trustees of any institution, struggling or not - to be sensitive to and aware of as due diligence is performed during the presidential search process.

Part One: Do Presidents Make a Difference?

This book is about presidents who "salvaged" their institutions by turning them around when they were in dire straits. We argue that these presidents made a difference. However, the literature on presidents in higher education does not assume that all presidents make a difference. The purpose of Part One is to place our "tales of turnarounds" in the context of the research to date on the impact of college and university presidents on their institutions. Does the research support the assertion that some presidents can/do make a difference? If indeed they can/do make a difference, what strategies do they employ? What kind of backgrounds did they bring to the president's desk? What personal stresses and strains do they experience? These are some of the basic questions for which we sought answers in the literature on higher education. They are also some of the basic questions for which we sought answers in our research on "salvaging presidents."

The Literature on Struggling Institutions

The literature on struggling institutions of higher education is abysmally limited. Burton Clark (1970) provided some historical insight in The Distinctive College: Reed, Antioch, and Swarthmore, in which he described the role of Arthur E. Morgan, who led Antioch to a new beginning, William T. Foster, the founding president of Reed, and Frank Aydelotte, the transforming president of Swarthmore. While Clark's study is valuable, it covered only three private institutions and described the work of presidents several generations ago.

Hamlin and Hungerford (1988) also provided some insight when they asked presidents to rank the tools that had been most effective in overcoming a financial crisis. However, their study was limited to financial issues and therefore did not include the full range of issues faced by the presidents in our study nor did they explore the backgrounds, skills, and personalities of the presidents who had to address that full range of issues. Their study is discussed in the context of our findings in Part Five.

Leslie and Fretwell (1996) initiated a study of thirteen institutions that encompassed the then extant Carnegie Classification except for Baccalaureate I; their research included one institution in our study, Tusculum College. They undertook this effort to test the validity of a fear that the two historic commitments of American higher education - providing universal access to post-secondary education and maintaining world-class leadership in the advancement of knowledge - might not be · sustainable. Their study is discussed in the context of our findings in Part Five.

Sellers (2005) reported on his early 1990 survey of 1,312 administrators and board chairs of 133 small colleges in various stages of decline or closure, coupled with subsequent interviews over the years with administrators of institutions that had closed. He concluded that there were controllable and uncontrollable factors that led to the closures, identified actions that the decline precipitated, and suggested possible responses. His study is discussed further in the context of our findings in Part Five.

The only in-depth description of a college turnaround that we have found is that by Keller (2004). He described the transformation of Elon College (NC) from "a small, unattractive, parochial bottom-feeder" institution in 1973, 90 percent tuition-dependent, a $3 million endowment against a $3.4 million indebtedness, offering only a baccalaureate degree to an enrollment, stuck for years, of 1,800 students, mainly from North Carolina and southern Virginia, with SATs of 750 to 1000. Now, Elon University has national recognition in being among the 300 finest undergraduate institutions in the country offering baccalaureate, masters, and doctoral degrees to an enrollment of 4,950 students from forty-eight states and with a mean SAT of 1159, all the while maintaining a tuition discount of only 12 percent against the national range of 25 to 45 percent or higher. Keller attributes the transformation to six factors: President Fred Young's mantra of "quality everywhere" (Young was President from 1973 to 1999); addiction to planning; attention to the selection, training, and rewarding of people; creating a distinctive niche among American colleges and universities; acumen about financing growth with relatively small amounts of its own money; and skill in marketing.

Although Kerr and Gade (1986), Cohen and March (1974), and Birnbaum (1988) all indicated that presidents in struggling institutions can make a difference, none provided specific examples of such presidents or institutions. Hence their studies are of limited value in assessing what strategies enabled the turnaround.

It is our anticipation that the shortcomings of this very limited literature on "salvaging presidents" will be abated by the analysis of our survey of such presidents and, most notably, by the in-depth interviews with the nine presidents who represent a cross-section of institutional types.

The Difference Presidents Make Today

The research by Bensimon, Birnbaum, and Neumann (1989) based on data from the thirty two institutions in the Institutional Leadership Project (Neumann and Bensimon 1990) is both hopeful and cautionary. The research suggests that presidents can make a difference today when they are exemplary instrumental and interpretive leaders attuned to the organizational culture, using multiple frames or cognitive complexity, working with teams, articulating the mission and managing meaning, and making choices that move the institution gradually in new directions consistent with institutional history and values.

However, it is unrealistic and undesirable to seek a return to the "giants" or "monarchs" of a century ago. As Birnbaum (1992) noted: "...[T]he plaintive query, Where have all the great leaders of the past gone? has an elementary answer: They are dead, along with the simpler times in which formal leaders could wield unbridled power to get what they wanted"(p.xii).

Unlike the bygone era in which some presidents were "giants" or "monarchs," higher education in the 21st century exists in different world, one characterized by participatory governance, shared influence, conflicting constituencies, and other complexities such as Federal, State, and System mandates and requirements, affirmative action or lack thereof, accommodating the disabled, amongst others. Few if any presidents today appoint the faculty, decide the curriculum, and teach students. Those who look for presidents who are "strong" in that sense will look in vain. But, as we will note in what follows from our study, presidents can make a difference in struggling institutions as leaders who learn the culture of their institution as well as where the mine fields are, plan and strategize, assemble a team of diverse mind sets, and recognize and motivate broader leadership within the institution. By a very different historical route than was the case in Europe, presidents in American colleges and universities have become "first among equals" on their campuses. In this role, a president can still make a difference and lead in new directions - not by fiat, and not alone, but as part of an institution that has a value and a role in society that is far greater than any individual who serves it.

This review of the scant literature on salvaging presidents and what follows from our survey and in-depth interviews indicate that turnaround leaders can make and have made a difference. How presidents in general make a difference on today's campuses is less clear, but the opportunity remains. The presidents in our study did make a difference and turned around their respective institutions, keeping them not only afloat but often piloting them in new directions.

Part Two: The Stories of Nine Presidents

We invited ten presidents to serve as case studies in order to provide further insight into the issues covered by the survey. The ten individuals were selected on the basis of the survey responses with an eye to encompassing the range of different types of Carnegie institutions. Inasmuch as the project was self-funded, convenience of access was also a factor in selecting the president for an interview. This resulted in five of the ten institutions being on the West Coast, four on the East Coast while one of us was there on other business, and one in the Midwest whose former president had retired to the Seattle, Washington area.

The presidents were interviewed by Kormondy, who sent the transcripts of the interviews back to the presidents for review and emendation. Unfortunately, one very engaging and commanding interview with the president of one of the East Coast baccalaureate colleges that provided a quite different perspective because of the person's background was withdrawn by the president herself on the advice of the board chair. Hence there are nine interviews presented here. It is also unfortunate that only one of the several public institution presidents, a community college, agreed to be interviewed.

Part Two presents the in-depth interviews in each president's own words. The format of each section is as follows: a brief background of the institution, a biographical sketch of the president/chancellor, and then the interview. The interviews were open-ended and qualitative, streams of consciousness as the presidents recalled, usually not in any chronological or systematic order, their rich experiences. This necessitated some occasional repositioning of the commentary to tie to the topic then at hand. An occasional prompt refocused the conversation, and the only consistent similarity at the end of each interview was a response to the question: Would you do it again?

The sequence of the nine sections is as follows (Carnegie Classification 2000 in parentheses) :

1. Dr. Donald F. Averill, Palo Verde College (Associates)

2. Dr. Thomas E. J. deWitt, Lasell College (Baccalaureate/Associates)

3. Dr. Peggy A. Stock, Colby-Sawyer College (Baccalaureate General)

4. Dr. Jerry C. Lee, National University (Masters I)

5. Dr. Robert E. Knott, Tusculum College (Masters II)

6. Dr. Garry D. Hays, United States International University (Doctoral Research Intensive)

7. Dr. Alan E. Guskin, Antioch University (Doctoral Research Intensive)

8. Dr. Stephen C. Morgan, University of La Verne (Doctoral Research Intensive)

9. Mr. Neil J. Hoffman, Otis College of Art and Design (Specialized - Art)

Dr. Donald F. Averill, Palo Verde College

The Institution

Palo Verde College, founded in 1946 and located in Blythe, California, is a state/local Associates College with about 5,000 students.

The College, established first on the site of the former Morton Air Academy, six miles Northwest of Blythe, opened as a junior college within the Palo Verde Unified School District with seventeen students and five teachers. In 1958, it moved into a Spanish style building on East Hobsonway. Athletics came into prominence but were eliminated in 1978 when the major support of the College was transferred by law [Proposition 13] from the local tax base to the State. The College moved to its present location, adjacent to a high school and middle school, in 1967 and separated from the Unified School District in 1969; however, it operated under a joint board until 1973 when a five-member, elected-at-large, Board of Trustees was created. At that time, the instructional program expanded to include vocational-technical, developmental, and continuing education courses. Growth expanded rapidly during the 1990s when Chuckawalla Prison opened nearby. The College purchased 200 acres for relocation by the fall of 2000.

The 1996-2001 mission statement denotes the College as "...an open access, public educational district, dedicated to providing excellence in education, cultural enrichment, economic development, and services to assist members of the community to meet their educational goals." The primary educational functions include: transfer education, vocational/occupational education, associate degree and certificate programs, and developmental education. In support of these functions, the College provides learning services (e.g., library, media), student services, basic skills development, continuing education, adult education, and community service

Upon appointment in 1996, Donald F. Averill became the ninth president. The longest in tenure, George W. Pennell, served nine years. Averill's immediate permanent predecessor, Wilford Biumel, served eight years (1987 - 1995); an interim president, Robert Wilmoth, served from 1995 to 1996. Dr. Averill resigned in 2000 to become Chancellor of the San Bernardino Community College District.

Donald F. Averill

Donald Averill pursued General Education at Los Angeles Valley College (Van Nuys, CA) and Business Administration at Los Angeles City College before receiving a BA in 1960 in Business Education and Health Education from California State University-Los Angeles, where he also received a MA in School Administration in 1965. He received the General Administration Credential from the University of Southern California in 1967 and a EdD in School Management from the University of La Verne in 1982.

Averill's administrative experience, all in California, includes: Coordinator, Work Experience Education, Whittier Union High School District (1967-72); Director, Career Education, Huntington Beach Union High School District (1972-77); Vice Chancellor, Educational Planning, Coast Community College District (1977-84); Dean, Area 1, Coastline Community College, Corona del Mar (1984-85); and Dean of Instruction, Career Education (1985-90) and Administrative Dean, Human Resources (1990-96), Glendale Community College.

His teaching experience includes the secondary level (1960-67) and subsequently California State Universities at San Luis Obispo, Fullerton, Long Beach, and Los Angeles (where he was an Associate Professor), and the University of California - Los Angeles.

Averill has served as a board member, officer, or committee chair of a number of professional associations (*e.g.,* Association of California Community College Administrators, American Association of Community and Junior Colleges) and community organizations (*e.g.,* Blythe Area Chamber of Commerce, Glendale Chamber of Commerce) and has had extensive experience as a chair or member of accreditation teams.

Donald Averill's comments that follow are a transcript of his interview on August 19, 1999 in his office at Palo Verde College. The questions that prompted his comments have either been omitted or are indicated within brackets.

The Situation and the Turnaround

I came to Palo Verde College knowing it was in trouble, so I was not surprised. But, it wasn't until after I arrived that I found out how severe the problems were. As you know, sometimes Boards don't tell you everything. Nonetheless, I had been warned that there was a possibility of the College being put on probation, and, eleven days after I arrived, the magic letter arrived from the Commission [Accrediting Commission for Community and Junior Colleges of the Western Association of Schools and Colleges (WASC)] saying we were being put on probation and had six months to come up with an interim plan for solving the problems.

There were basically five issues, some of them very serious. One of the charges was that the Board was materially involved in micromanaging the District [Palo Verde Community College District]. A good example of that is that my predecessor resigned the day after the accreditation team visit in March, and the five member Board literally ran the District until I arrived in June. They had two new Board members, who had not had any board training, and they were just going wild - they were attending meetings of faculty and students, literally interfering with the operation of the school and telling people they couldn't do this and do that. The second charge was that the College had a catalogue that didn't reflect the offerings of the school. Many courses were being offered that were not in the catalog, and many that were in the catalog were not being offered. Course outlines were totally out-of-date. They had a policies and procedures manual that was undistinguishable, some of which wasn't picked up in the accreditation process. Further, they had not completed their educational master plan. Those were the major things.

This was the surface stuff that was in the accreditation report. When we got into the setting, not only was that taking place, but with a total of twenty-one faculty, there were six major pieces of litigation, one of which was at the arbitration level. There was in-fighting among constituencies, with faculty wanting me to fire all the administrators and get rid of two Board members, and Board members wanting me to fire five of the faculty. However, I decided not to fire anybody and, instead, try to work things out.

When I started looking at where the College was, I realized that they had not had any leadership. President Biumel, who had been here for eight years, appeared to have done very well in the early years, but then he decided he wanted to build a new campus, started working with an architect, and reached a point in 1994 when he could have started construction. However, in that year, while the College was still in the queue, the State ran out of construction funds. The State sent out a notice that they had run out of money and asked for justification as to why the College should be left in the line; but, he never answered, and the College was moved out of the queue.

Then he decided he would just save money out of current budgets, so he started peppering it away, not giving money to anyone. If something broke, he would manage to get by. As a result, in about two years (from before 1994 to 1996), he stashed away five million dollars, and by the time I arrived, the College had a six million dollar reserve. But, he was letting everything else go. Then, in the last few years, several faculty and Board members started going after him, and he started giving the store away. One of the most damaging things is that he left the faculty believing that anytime the State gave a COLA [cost of living adjustment] to the district, they would automatically receive the raise. And yet, he prides himself on his negotiation skills. It was this that led up to the fighting with Biumel, with faculty members taking sides, Board members taking sides. As a result, morale was in the absolute pits.

There were a couple of things I started to look at immediately, among them the litigation issues. There were two students who had civil rights claims against the District; there were three faculty members who had charges against them, one by a student, one by an administrator, and another that had started as a grievance by another faculty member. When I looked at the contents of all those pieces, it was obvious that no one had tried to mediate. So, I brought the parties in and, except for the civil rights matters, got them closed within six months, deciding there were no issues. For example, one concerned a faculty member who had been reprimanded for shouting at an administrator. They had been dealing with the matter for a long time, and all they were trying to do was to put a letter in his file, a letter that would have been effective for only six months. So, I finally asked the Board if it wanted to spend $20,000 just to put a letter in the faculty member's file for six months. Of course, they said 'No,' and so we closed the issue. The civil rights matter, however, necessitated some major restructuring of the discrimination and sexual harassment policies.

For the faculty, there is heightened concern about due process, so we have to be very careful when developing or revising any policy that we address due process properly.

I will tell you that it wasn't smooth sailing because, in the middle of this, I was letting a couple of faculty off the hook; at least one administrator, if not more, did not agree with my procedure - one of them was my vice president who started undermining things in the process, a game plan that has irritated a number of faculty. We still have not totally resolved this, but we have come to terms on it.

In terms of replacing or terminating people, I did nothing of the sort. We had one Board member retire when her term expired, and the replacement lasted only a year because he was working for the prison system and was reassigned, so we had to make a new appointment. In fact, we have not laid off anybody, including the five faculty members known as dissidents. I had become extremely adroit in what I call 'canal diplomacy.' I would take people out for a walk along the canal; they would yell, and I would yell. By the time we ended the walk, we would come to some compromise and move forward.

As for the Board, we resolved matters with the three trustees who had been highly involved in micromanagement. The resolution came through board training based, in part, on my human resources background. I had a fairly firm understanding of the Brown Act, which stipulates the procedures to be followed in California for open meetings by legislators and public agencies. It wasn't that they had not had training as a Board because the California Community College League had come here three or four times before I got here. They hired Bill Corey from the League, and he did the search when I has hired and had worked with them a couple of other times on various issues. I had Corey come out afterwards to do an assessment of the Board after the first year of operation, and then I started getting some Board members to California Community College Trustees meetings, and that worked miracles.

There are two doctors on the board, a radiologist and a general practitioner. When I came on board, one of them would come to Board meetings with a stack of medical records and would sit there and make medical notes throughout the whole meeting. After I got him to a Board orientation, there was a dramatic change. The rest of them, including the new member, who have gone to Board orientations are doing marvelously.

The real problem is that both Biumel and Wilmouth did not communicate directly with the Board but rather would talk only to the president of the Board so the other Board members didn't know what was going on half of the time. Now, the Board receives a Friday letter every week, and we go over everything that is happening - good, bad, and indifferent. The only thing I don't put in are any personnel matters since that would become a matter of public record.

The Board meets once a month for business sessions plus seven study sessions over the year. We began regular meetings, setting Board goals, getting them to evaluate themselves - they had not evaluated themselves in God knows how long. I can say quite honestly that is is a wholly different Board than the one that hired me, but with only one new member, and about that I feel very good. We turned it around.

We had a difficult time getting people focused on the seriousness of the accreditation issues. It took us eighteen months to get off probation. At first, there was a constituency that thought losing accreditation was no big thing because they believed the State would just assign us to another college. And, both sides thought if we would get rid of the schlock around here, all our problems would be solved. I've worked with accreditation for twenty-four years, done thirty-two accreditation visits - in other words, I know the system. Based on my accreditation experience, I informed the constituents that WASC does not accredit districts, they accredit colleges, and you've got to understand that if you lose accreditation, it will take three years before you can get re-accredited. Then Dave Wolf [David B. Wolf was then Executive Director of WASC's Commission on Community and Junior Colleges.] visited and told them exactly what I had been saying. We met with each of the constituencies individually, and it finally sunk in.

I think the key part of the problem I had, particularly with the vice president, was that I was willing to listen to faculty concerns and to indicate they really ought to have a voice in how we solve the problems. He felt that we had done that, and that you ultimately tell them that's it and you just go forward. I countered that you did try that, and it got you on probation. So, the final turning point was that I agreed with the CTA [California Teachers Association] group that we would use a group of their people to mediate the development of the education master plan. We used a process called Future Research. It was not developed by CTA but instead was a community and business model, but they had a group who had gone through the Future Research training and who could facilitate those types of meetings. So, the College brought them in, and we started to do the plan.

The key strategy I wanted to use was to move away from internal constituencies. We needed the support of the community. So we brought in the Unified School District, prisons, Chamber of Commerce, City of Blythe staff, and students from the Unified School District, as well as our own. It was eye-opening to some of the faculty that there really were some directions in which the community wanted to go. One of the things the faculty has never been excited about was the new campus. They found out the community really wanted it, and now that lack of interest on the part of the faculty is set aside, and we are all working on it.

In fiscal year 1994-95, the College had 850 FTE students; in 1995-96, the year in which all the major in-fighting occurred, everyone in town backed away from the College, and the FTE dropped to 621. There was another factor tied into that: Biumel had started selling his over-cap ADA [Average Daily Attendance] to other districts. He was not alone in that maneuver - some twenty-eight districts were caught in the review by the Legislative Analyst's Office. Basically, they were working with public safety agencies, doing training for them. But the agencies were staffing the programs, and the districts were collecting the apportionment money.

When I came in, I said we are not going to play that game, and that if we are to be involved in public safety programs, we will do it by the law. As a result, we took a big hit in that year. That has all been retrieved, and the past year we had 956 FTE students. That number reflects a significant growth in public safety training but under proper procedures. Biumel had never gone to WASC to tell them he was doing this program, so he was really violating the accreditation agreement. I prepared a supplemental report on those programs to WASC, which gave its blessing, and we've reported to the State that we were following the guidelines.

The District also cut an agreement with Riverside Community College to set up a consortium with the Ben Clark Training Center so that both Colleges could offer programs through that Center. It is generating close to 250 FTE students every year, all legitimately.

When I first looked at the data for the College, one of the things that shocked me was that the proportion of males was 72% in contrast to the average community college, which is 44%. Part of the explanation was the public safety outreach program because being public safety meant it was primarily male. The other thing that caught me was that the average student load was three units; again, this was due to the same program in which students enrolled for two units, pulling down the average. I really wanted to cut that back and get some growth in the local area.

When I looked into the agreements that the College made at the time it separated from the Unified School District in 1969, I discovered that the College was granted the right to offer non-credit courses but had not done so for about five years. So, we re-instituted the non-credit program, which is now generating seventy FTE students and will be well over 100 to 200 in the next year or two. So we now see ourselves as serving the community.

Originally the faculty were not really happy with me about this, primarily because they were operating a strong ESL [English as a Second Language] program. When the non-credit program was put in, it siphoned off folks who were not really working at a credit level. The faculty saw their enrollments go down. However, it has started to balance now. We are beginning to develop a matriculation program so that those folks just don't disappear after they get some language capacity to function at the college level and instead matriculate into college progams. I think in a year or two that concern will have died.

I prepared an initial environmental scan before I came on board to determine whether the College did have the potential to survive, and I presented it to the Board at the interview; after I was on board, the scan was updated. Initially I wanted to see what the potential was for growth, economic development, and so on; when the pieces were put together it seemed salvageable.

There were two things that really drew me to the job: putting a new campus together that would be on the technology cutting edge and trying to produce a program that would give people the same access that they would have if they lived in a metropolitan area. We have made good strides in that direction.

Right now we have two four-year colleges that are working with the community - CSU [California State University]-Chico and Park College in Missouri. Park is actually on the campus. When they first came in they said they needed a hundred students to sustain the program, but they have stuck with us although there are only about thirty students enrolled. I think that with the new campus opening up, it will open other doors for them. Also they have started offering on-line programs so more students are accessing it by the internet. But our biggest problem is that Park College is accredited by the North Central Association of Schools and Colleges, so we can't do teacher-credential programs. Thus we are working with CSU-San Bernardino to get on-line teacher training by telecourse. If that works, we will have access for people in that area.

Regarding the environmental scan, I looked at what was being done in education. For example, I looked at what was being done for the prison population. When the first prison, Chuckawalla, opened, there was a direct interface with the College to provide courses for the employees and prisoners. Somehow that got backed out - I am not sure whether my predecessor backed out or whether the prison backed out, because they do have a strong vocational program that they operate internally. But I saw that the College had not tried to develop a working relationship to develop programs for their employees. This has since been resolved.

I looked at the farm community and found the College had done absolutely nothing programmatically for it. That was a tougher nut to crack than I thought it would be, but we are now doing some things.

I looked at the fact that there was an opportunity to do some diversity in economic development, and as a result of that, we have entered into a partnership with the City of Blythe in which the College is actually running the Small Business Economic Development Center [SBEDC] for the City. It also became the location for our non-credit program since we were running out of space for both the credit and non-credit programs. So the City gave us a building for a dollar a year, and we created another seven classrooms, a conference room, and working offices for an incubator system. We now have our first incubator in operation at the Center.

I looked at the growth potential for the community and recognized that it needed economic diversity. The College is now stimulating this effort through the Small Business Center [SBEDC] for the City. The Center was instrumental in working with Riverside County to get funding for an 'Empowerment Zone' through the U. S. Department of Agriculture for $4 million. Other grants have also been acquired amounting to over $85,000.

After I got here, I started meeting with all the constituent groups and finally got very active with them. They had what was called the Palo Verde Valley Economic Partnership, a group composed of the larger utilities, Chamber of Commerce, City of Blythe, and others. They were funding the partnership from the 'bed tax' from the motels, which generates about $6,000 a year, spending this on an annual economic outlook conference, a 'show and tell' for Riverside County. The county farmers come in and have a day of speeches and meetings, then eveyone goes home. I can't say it has been non-productive because they did get the County to put in a new County center in town about a year ago, and they reconstructed the Superior Court building. The Partnership was able to get the County to give the City control of the airport. This all opened up our working relationship with the City to swing the direction of the Partnership to really address an economic model.

To bring the community back into the College, I first note that my predecessors had never tried working with the City. When I came in I met with the City fathers, Council, and City Manager, and we started conversing with each other. As a result of that activity, we established a joint council that meets once a year that includes the Unified School District, City Council, me, and our Board. I knew I had to get them back into the fold to move the College forward. I also knew I had to mend fences with the Unified District, so I started meeting with the staff to patch the wounds that had been created.

One of the things that happened in the first year was that the City came to the College and asked if we could help in constructing a house. Since we had a construction program, we agreed to help, and we did it. They provided the supplies and property, and we supplied the labor in a partnership. We are starting our second house this year.

So, it was communication and openness. It's what I call putting the community back into the term community college - we were identifying their needs and developing programs that could get us there and bring us closure. I have been active in the Chamber of Commerce and am presently President-Elect; I am currently President of the Partnership. All this is what brought the community back to us.

Regarding the planning for the Future Research at the UCLA facilities at Lake Arrowhead, the leaders of the faculty were cooperating with us because I was using their people. Had I brought in any other resource, I think there would have been a problem getting cooperation from them. Because it was a CTA [California Teachers Association] program, they were really behind it. However, there was a lot of resistance from at least two of my Board members until they participated in the event. After it was over, it was a totally different thing. They realized that the facilitators were really acting as facilitators and did not have any hidden agendas. The other unhappy group was the classified staff because they perceived that I was listening only to the faculty since everything revolved around a CTA solution. That was something I had to overcome, and I knew that if I didn't get everyone directed to where they wanted the College to go, we couldn't play anything.

The next thing was to get the model set for program review, one of the five areas the faculty had done nothing about. That was a hostile situation as well because the interim president had drawn up a model that the faculty wouldn't sign off on although other constituencies had. His attitude was that it should be stuffed down their throats and for them to live by it. Conversely, the faculty had gone to the statewide Academic Senate, which gave them a model that had been used at Chabot College. It was evident that they weren't going to accept the administration's model, and it was equally evident to me that the Chabot model wasn't going to work in a small institution. So we scrapped it and started over again. That's when I started 'canal diplomacy' with the faculty leader and said there was no way you could use the Chabot model because you don't have enough people to make that model work. So we finally got them to look at other small institutions like Tahoe and Kern, and we came up with a compromise model that is now being used. We are starting our third iteration of program review, the ones to date having been relatively successful based on the resources we had to do those reviews.

One of the key problems that is now just getting resolved is that the College had no MIS [Management Information System]. When I arrived, what was used was based on an IBM System 36, which had not been produced since 1967; it is still being used. If we don't have this turned around by January 1, we will really have trouble. We brought the Technology Committee together, interviewed several vendors, and selected a service provider that will operate off the internet with everything coming out of Phoenix, Arizona. In fact, they are starting to do the installation today and will start staff training so we can run parallel systems during the fall semester with, hopefully, roll-over to the new system in the spring. With the current system, any time we really want to look at data, it requires us to do it by hand so it has been tough to do program reviews.

The only area from the accreditation review that we have not resolved is institutional research. They had made a recommendation, as has the State's matriculation people, that we have an institutional researcher on the staff. However, with all the other needs and priorities of the institution, that is one thing I decided we have to forego until we can afford it. We need to do something because next year we will be starting the next iteration for an accreditation visit, and the new accreditation model is highly accountability-centered.

Is there complete peace and harmony on the campus now? No, and if there were, it would be a very unusual campus. We are still working at it. A couple of areas we are working on include a policy and procedures manual, which just about blew me out of my mind when I started searching for regulations - it was a hodge-podge. The matter that caused the civil rights problem I discussed earlier was that there were three different policies about discrimination and sexual harassment. However, it is finally getting to be a pretty clean piece of work.

The catalog was a complete disaster. When we got into it, we got into graduation standards during which the faculty could not reach closure. I finally intervened because the direction they were heading would only have been an A.S. degree and nothing to handle the liberal arts side of the house. About a third of the faculty comes out of Arizona, and Arizona has an A.A.S. degree, which California does not - we call them certificates.

It just boggles my mind that the Education Code is written so loosely that there can be seventy interpretations of what a transfer degree is supposed to look like. So faculty were going off in all directions. For example, the business department did not want to have intermediate algebra as a requirement because they thought they would lose students. But, I reminded them that if graduates of the program wanted to get a CPA, they are going to have to meet that college math requirement someplace.

There is an interesting observation I would make based on the institutions in which I have worked, that is, you have about five or six faculty who are going to be tough no matter what. But here, that five or six made up 20 percent of the faculty - an analog to China's Gang of Four. This group holds the organizational power because the base group will not go against them. Unfortunately, a lot of their direction was not based on a good sound rationale. But, nobody wants to confront them. That is changing, however, since I have brought in new faculty who are not as apathetic about matters. But, they are still in a leadership role. The same two people have switched on and off being the union president since I arrived. I don't see how the faculty puts up with one of them because her process of getting things done is to stonewall; so when she doesn't agree with you, she just won't give an answer. This was driving the previous administration crazy. I have finally found ways to push stuff around her. This year, the faculty got unhappy with her because she withheld her 'openers' for bargaining for three-quarters of the year. Thus we would not have been able to bring closure to negotiations unless they wanted to bargain through the summer, so they removed her as president.

There is another component. One of the things I discovered when I came out here is that the District had not only isolated itself from the State, the State had isolated itself from the District. There was no communication going on about this District at all. A conscious effort was made to work with the Chancellor's Office and to stay active with the California Community College Trustees and the State administrative association, of which I will be president in two years. Now they know that Blythe and Palo Verde Community College are here.

When Wilmoth was appointed interim president, the faculty went ballistic because the Board did it without opening it up. And the State did one of those interfering things they shouldn't have done and made the Board stop the process. Wilmoth was a candidate for the permanent position, but half way through he pulled out because he had been censured by the Academic Senate.

One of the good things I can say about the faculty is that most are very good teachers, but there are one of two who are crummy teachers, and something needs to be done about that. They did not have a good evaluation system. It is ironic that when I got here, out of nine measures in AB 1725, which established clear priorities for the community colleges, they had completed only one - that on retreat rights for administrators - even though they were so mad at the administration. However, during the past three years, we have completed all of the measures.

Would you do it again?

If I could see this far down the line, I would probably say yes. Had I known beforehand as much as I did after I got into it, I don't know. That would be the real question. There were some really tough personality conflicts. The other problem I had is that my wife was not really happy about my coming out here from my position in Glendale and our home in Orange County, so we had a commuter marriage for three years. Carol had just a few years before she was to retire, and had she come out here she would have taken a considerable loss in pay. In that first year, I told her there is no Hell - I live in it! In retrospect, it was probably a benefit because I could work late at night and not be in the position of ignoring her.

Dr. Thomas E. J. deWitt, Lasell College

The Institution

Lasell College, founded in 1851 and located in Newton, Massachusetts, is an independent, non-profit Baccalaureate/Associate's College with about 1,200 students.

In the mid-1800's, Edward Lasell, a graduate and later professor of chemistry at Williams College, was impressed with the quality of scholarship exhibited by women while he was on leave teaching at Mount Holyoke Seminary [later College]. As a result, he established Auburndale Female Seminary in 1851. A year later, after his death, it was renamed in his honor as Lasell Female Seminary. At its founding, Lasell was, along with Harvard University, the only other institution of higher learning in the greater Boston area as well as the nation's oldest private two-year college for women. It held the latter distinction until 1989 when it was granted approval to award four-year degrees. After 1865, when the Lasell family ended its control, the Seminary was led for over seven decades by three principals/presidents, Charles W. Cushing, Dr. Charles Bragdon, and Dr. Guy Winslow. Adoption of the name Lasell Junior College came in 1932, the Junior being dropped in 1989. Admission of men began in September, 1998.

From the outset, Lasell emphasized both the practical and the scholarly, departing radically from the "finishing school" attitude then prevalent in the 19th century. For example, it was the first college to offer courses that developed into programs for nutritionists and dieticians, the first to establish a retailing department, and among the first, if not the first, of women's colleges to build a gymnasium and swimming pool and establish a physical education department.

The College's mission is "...to provide a stimulating environment for the intellectual and personal growth of students" and encompasses three significant opportunities for all students: outstanding professional and liberal arts programs with an emphasis on integration of the two; activities that translate classroom theory to professional practice; and a small, diverse community that fosters strong interpersonal relationships and a supportive living and learning environment. In fulfilling its mission, the College is guided by three core values: student focus, innovative education, and social responsibility. In its Plan 2001, the College anticipated offering selected masters degrees.

Upon appointment in 1988, Thomas E. J. deWitt became the twelfth president (including five principals). The longest in tenure, Guy M. Winslow, served thirty-nine years (twenty-four as the last principal, 1908-1932, and fifteen as president, 1932-47). President deWitt's immediate predecessor, Peter Mitchell, served five years. Thomas deWitt retired as President in June, 2007.

Thomas E. J. deWitt

Thomas deWitt received a BA (*Summa cum laude*) in 1967 from the University of Manitoba, a MA and PhD in 1971 from the University of Virginia, and a MBA in Public Management (high honors) in 1979 from Boston University.

From 1971-77, he served as Visiting Assistant Professor of History at Queen's University, University of Manitoba, Wellesley College, and University of Toronto. He was Resource Planning Analyst at Tufts University (May through September 1978), Consultant to the City of Boston (June through August 1979), Director of Finance and Business, Regis College (1979-85), Vice President for Administration (1985-86) and Executive Vice President (1986-88), Endicott College.

Dr. deWitt, a member of Phi Beta Kappa and Beta Gamma Sigma, received Woodrow Wilson Doctoral and Dissertation Fellowships and has published on the Third Reich. He has served on accreditation teams for the New England Association of Schools and Colleges and on its Commission on Institutions of Higher Education. He has been a consultant to the American Optometric Association Council on Optometric Education and to small colleges as a member of NACUBO [National Association of College and University Business Officers], a past member of the

Beverly and Newton Rotary Clubs, and is active in church governance, including chairmanship of finance committees.

Thomas deWitt's comments that follow are a transcript of his interview on October 15, 1999 in his office. The questions that prompted his comments have either been omitted or are indicated within brackets.

The Situation and the Turnaround

I am in my twelfth year; I came here in 1988 because of experiences that happened before. I am an historian who later went back and got a MBA when it looked like tenure track jobs were not around. Also I had married my wife who was to become and still is a tenured professor at Wellesley College. So we knew we were very committed to the area, and I had had too many one year jobs to keep being a commuting husband. So, I gave that up after five years - it was too expensive, I had published too much, and no one was going to hire me anymore. So, I got the MBA and went into administration.

Three years before I came here will be somewhat telling of why I am here in the first place.

I had gone to Endicott College, which is up in the North Shore in Beverly, also a two-year women's college. Unbeknownst to me, it was on its very last legs - the bank was pulling the line of credit, and there was no money to pay the staff. So, we negotiated quickly since the bank knew me personally because I had done a rather intriguing bond issue with them at a prior institution. In three years, the College went from huge deficits to quadrupling its endowment and building dormitories. It was a success story. And, of course, its number one competitor was Lasell. I was tired of the long commute from the North Shore all the way to Wellesley and had a young son with whom I wanted to spend more time.

Then, this job came along, and I took it even though I recognized the institution was in trouble. I did due diligence as I had not done at Endicott. I had learned a lesson at Endicott by not having asked what condition the school was in. Imagine going to Endicott and a week later getting a call from the bank saying it was not renewing your line of credit! Thus, when I was considering going to Lasell, I asked for financial and enrollment information, which I found alarming. But, when I got here I found the institution was in worse shape than most of the trustees recognized, although some of them had a sense. A couple of the trustees were financial people who, by some miracle, had been brought onto the Board either because of distant relatives who had graduated from here or some other personal connection.

When I first interviewed with the Board, I told them they didn't know their market well and, if they continued the present course, the College would be going out of business. Further, I told the Board that the College needed to change course dramatically. After conveying that bleak information, I was surprised by being invited back and that I was to be accompanied by my wife. I was one of three finalists, two of them very prominent women. One of the women was on the Boston Vault, a trustee at Regis (so I knew her), and a senior vice president at Filene's [an upscale Boston Department store]; the other was Provost of George Mason University. Although historically a women's college, Lasell had never had a woman president.

There were 25 trustees at the interview, but a lot of the former trustees who were alums and who would never vote for a woman as president were no longer on the Board. During the interview I again reiterated my position about the fragility of the institution and what they needed to do about it. The Vice Chairman of the Board turned to me and said, 'We've already heard that from you before,' turned to my wife, and said, 'Dr. Ward, is he always like this.' She said, 'The first time I met him I couldn't stand him.' That broke up the Board and broke the ice.

The institution was facing its third consecutive deficit, ten percent or $560,000 of its operating budget, $300,000 the year before, and $100,000 the year before that. The College also began the year with a thirty-year low in enrollment. At its height, it had 900 students; it was never very large given that it is constrained within the neighborhood. It looked pretty grim.

My predecessor, who was here for five years, started off in great style, was very personable, very charming, and had some fundraising ability but lacked management skills. He tried to stop the decline of his predecessor but was only marginally successful. He wanted to leave, and so did the Board, so he left under mutual agreement.

We were in tough shape. We had millions of dollars of deferred maintenance and were just beginning to put some computers in some classrooms, although in 1988 that was the early phase nationally. Faculty had been laid off, thankfully my predecessor did that, I didn't. The place was hemorrhaging. This decline was particularly hard for what was at one time a very interesting and quite acclaimed institution. To be sure, it was a little bit like a finishing school, but different. The reality was that it used to draw students from around the world - Hong Kong, Malaysia, Europe, Hawaii, and all over the country. They used to advertise nationally, even in the *New York Times*. It had its hey day in the mid 30's to late 40's. It was quite something. And, for young women who did not need that much education, Lasell was a good place. But, like so many institutions, it didn't change - it felt it could simply rely on that name recognition. When everyone introduced four-year degrees in recognition that a two-year degree in the 80's and today doesn't go very far, this College just absolutely stubbornly refused to change. They brought consultants, one from the University of Massachusetts-Amherst, to do an analysis of the College in 1982-83, and they determined that they should go back to being a two-year college with a college-prep program by having grades 11-12, which Lasell did have at one time.

Keep in mind that this is an institution in which Winston Churchill spoke, where U.S. presidents came, and to which Robert Frost dedicated a poem. It had its day in the sun. Therefore it was very hard to give up that illustrious history and become more market driven. In fact, much of its success in the 30's and 40's as well as into the 50's and 60's came because it began to respond to some market changes, whether it was in retailing or an associates degree nursing program, the only one in New England, which ultimately accounted for over half of the student population in its hey day.

Call it stubbornness, it refused to change. When I came, its endowment was down to $3 million. In spite of its deficits, it was trying to upgrade its buildings, but since it had no money, it largely took it out of the endowment. My predecessor's predecessor had balanced the budget each year by selling College property. We owned nearly two-thirds of the Auburndale neighborhood; we owned a great deal of this portion of Newton. We have sold easily ten to fifteen houses, estates, and large tracts of land. The budget was balanced each year between 1977 and 1983 when President Arthur M. Griffin was here. But clearly, the Board was not sufficiently engaged or someone might have said you don't balance your budget by selling capital or that you might sell it to reinvest it but not to pay operating expenses.

Peter Mitchell, my immediate predecessor, turned some of that around. He invigorated or really began fundraising; they had never raised any real money. They had an annual fund and one campaign, to build a swimming pool, raising two or three hundred thousand dollars in the 1970's. Peter Mitchell was the first president to appreciate the importance of fundraising and a market-driven admissions program, having spent his professional career in both capacities at two-year colleges. Single-handedly, he raised $1.3 million in a capital campaign - that was quite something. Unfortunately, the College got in trouble again in his final years, and he layed off faculty and staff. When I came, there was only one person left in the entire development, communications, public relations, alumnae affairs, and annual fund area - one person, a secretary. And he told me there was no way to raise money - that Lasell was 'topped out.' The College had dated degrees, no cache of land, financial blood letting, and incredible declining because of the laying off of faculty and staff, a salary freeze, and a campus that, while it didn't look as bad as when Mitchell came, still looked pretty seedy.

Lots of things happened. With the experience of my MBA, I began to make some changes by literally starting to find out where the data were. There weren't any. We didn't even know who was on the payroll. Nobody controlled it. We had a vice president who was very good, but Peter Mitchell didn't let her do anything. He made all the decisions. So, it took a while to change it. Obviously having an MBA and some training in operations management and having turned Endicott around, we started. I didn't promise anything to the Board. I made my acceptance of the position conditional on them going four years, and that was understood. Without that I wouldn't come. They wanted to know how much it would cost, and I said I didn't have any idea. But, if you don't do it, you've got to survive anyway.

Over time, we made changes. They came slowly, but they came consistently. First, we started cutting expenses where we could, rationalizing, improving morale - and there were some significant things that happened that I will go back to - and immediately filing for a name change from Lasell Junior College to Lasell: A Two Year College for Women, just to get the Junior out of it. We started a process to determine which were our strongest majors - in the first round it was Education and Fashion.

Importantly, we began preparing the documentation for going four-year. This is probably the toughest State I am aware of in the nation for getting degree elevation. We had to go through a Board of Education run by the State - very rigorous - and I said to our Board that given our financial status, no State is going to give us approval to go four-year if we can't manage our business as a two-year institution. We need to raise some money. Ironically, I had also taken the job with two conditions - 1) that we go four-year and 2) that I did not have to raise any money.

We brought in the consultant who had conducted the original campaign who said people love Lasell but that it is an emotional attachment without intellectual engagement, that they felt good about their personal experiences but don't feel good about where it is today. He thought we could raise $1 million from the Board but that would be it. We would have to do ten or twenty other things to improve the infrastructure before we could have a real campaign. The Board signed on, and it was mostly Board members who dug deep - I'd say sixty percent of the money raised came from trustees. Three or four key alums also gave money.

The other change was a real emphasis on the business climate and making some tough business decisions. Before he left, my predecessor had begun another second mini-campaign to raise a half million dollars, which he was good at, and raised most of that money to it to convert an old building that had been a student center, which had been vacant for a decade or two, into a business center. He had this image that the College needed a business school with a fancy name, a kind of management center. In my first weeks getting to know this very large campus I found that one of its problems was that we must have had one of the largest capital infrastructures per student in the entire nation. We had forty-three buildings for 393 students! As I walked with the director of the physical plant, I asked what we used this classroom for, and he responded, 'We don't need this, so it is empty.' Again and again. So, I am thinking, why are we building a management center with six more classrooms? 'I don't know, but that's what Peter wanted.'

So, I got the Board to kill that and turn it into a teaching, day-care facility - because I had a young child who needed to go to one. We invested $400,000 to retrofit and do it over. It was a successful investment that yields some $200,000 a year. The Board perked up - a 50 percent return on investment. It was great publicity because, although we had a nursery school for many years at the other end of the campus, we didn't have a teaching day-care facility. As many more women go to work, the nursery school isn't deemed as practical since it was only a half-day program.

So, there was already a set change, and the Board felt that management systems were put in place. Trustees didn't meet independently with auditors before, but they do now. I get evaluated every year.

There were three distinct things I did very quickly that I think helped, and that

I'm sure is true of any institution to turn it around - is to get everybody on board and give everyone hope. For the Board, it was setting up the practice of sending them information every month from October through June. During July, August, and September, I do my annual report, and I may send them little updates. Everyone of these monthly reports is several pages long telling what is happening on campus so there are no surprises. It has some national information, enrollment information, fundraising information, and interesting articles from the *Chronicle* [*of Higher Education*] or elsewhere that educate the trustees about the role of higher education so they can better understand the issues facing colleges in general, not just Lasell. This has worked well; there were never any surprises. In years when it looks like enrollment isn't going to be good, I could report that concern in November, and every month I would repeat that mantra; in September when there was a 20 or 30 student drop in enrollment, no one was surprised. That brought enormous amounts of good will.

Secondly, I conceived of this retirement community, about which I will talk separately later. Everyone saw this as the linchpin of Lasell's recovery. However, it hasn't been that nor was it intended to be, but the fact that it was perceived by the community to be the thing that would save us is fine. It gave everyone hope.

Lastly, I rehired all but one of the faculty because I needed their good will in order to go four-year. You can't go four-year in an institution that is heavily a two-year faculty, very few terminally degreed, unless you can win them over. You can't threaten to fire them all.

The first year ended with a modest surplus instead of a $600,000 deficit. It was a modest surplus, but it was a surplus. And, we have never looked back since. That first year was absolutely critical both to our survival and to the new relationship that had developed between the administration and trustees, who had no longer trusted the last president. And, there was no love lost between the faculty and the administration by that time because the faculty felt they had been duped. It is not a unionized faculty, though I had had a unionized faculty at Endicott, and I would never have another one in my lifetime. It is difficult, and I have my own prejudices. But, we brought the faculty in and began to develop four-year programs, cut a deal with them, developed a very complicated, much too convoluted, huge document about transitions, and so on. Basically, I said the deal is you help me go four-year, and I will guarantee every faculty member's job whether they have a terminal degree or not. But, I am imposing terminal degree requirements on new faculty immediately in fields where you can reasonably get them. It doesn't mean business - we can't get a DBA - but, we should be able to get a PhD in English if a position opens up.

We had five visits in two years: the New England Commission, the State for two times, and another outside agency. I could not have written better reports myself - they were absolutely glowing. It was the fact that the staff rallied around – it wasn't people hiding behind the bushes saying let me tell you the real story. There wasn't any other story than the one they saw.

I think that has been the hallmark of the turnaround. I learned from my own mistakes but also from my role as the CFO in two institutions, which were very autocratic - one was Regis, a wonderful institution, but being run by Sisters, it has kind of mentality where the Sisters' curtains are yellow or green or whether we are going to paint the woodwork. True stories. It demotivated everyone, no one made a decision because you felt someone was looking over your shoulder and wondered what the president was going to say.

So, I had already said to myself that if I ever became a president - in fact, truly, I never wanted to be, and still don't want to be one, I would have been happy in a tenured position at a Toronto or Wellesley, where I had taught before - I would devolve authority. I make very few decisions, except the very biggest. I have had almost no turnover in twelve years in the entire senior staff except one for illness and one termination. Why? Because they are all 'presidents' - they have immense talent. When I go on the road for three or four weeks, I don't have to call in, I don't have to. If there is a crisis, they will handle it. If it is really bad, my Executive Assistant knows how to reach me. But, I don't believe in micromanaging - I take my projects on, they do the job of managing the place. There are no individual decisions. They are so powerful now that when we are in merger negotiations - we have been approached several times to take over small institutions - they constantly vote against it, and I constantly withdraw the proposal as a testimony as to how good they are. I am very proud of that aspect of the management structure.

We've had some problems this year with faculty. We are not the place we were. There is nothing other than the physical structure that is common to the institution it was in 1988 and the institution today. We are on the verge of a graduate school, we have the highest enrollment in twenty years, we are full for the first time in thirty, we have evicted every tenant, including me, from houses that we owned that were dormitories we didn't need. Among the advantages we had here when enrollment dropped, we could rent all these houses for $2,000 a month, so we picked up over $250,000 in rentals. Even the president had to be evicted because his house had been a dorm, so we had to find another house we owned, which is being retrofitted while we are temporarily in the President's quarters for a year.

We have invested $3 million in technology. This entire campus is connected underground by fiber. Every student has a "port per pillow" computer hookup, telephone hookup, and one cable connection per room. We have floated $12 million of bond issues to refinance a $3 million debt we took on three years ago, something we couldn't conceive of doing twelve years ago. We had to build a gymnasium, athletic facilities, and we had to start the computer investments. At this stage, we are the only college that Moody has ever given an investment grade rating that has less than a thousand students, and they renewed it when we floated the bond issue, though Lasell doesn't guarantee it, from $3 million to $12 million. And we are sponsors for a $58 million bond issue that closes on December 31st for the retirement center. Our endowment has gone from $3 million to $12 million, and fundraising has gone from 9 percent alumnae participation in 1988 to 28 percent. So, instead of raising $125,000 a year in the annual fund, we raise half a million now, with six consecutive annual increases.

More significantly, four years ago, I indicated that we were six years away from our 150th birthday in 2001 and that a year from now we have to start a solid case for a campaign. Frankly, I needed to do it because of a visit I made to the then Chairman of the Board - we change Chairs every four years - on Sanibel Island, Florida, his winter residence. He was the person who kept the place alive before I came; he was senior vice president, number two man, at a sales investment house in Boston, and his grandmother went here. When I arrived, his first question was, 'How's the fundraising going?' I knew that was my next job. We called back our fundraising consultants who estimated that we could raise $9 million now; which was such an odd number, I raised it to $10 million. We raised $8 million in the first eleven months of the silent phase and raised the goal to $12 million; we are almost at that level now and still have two years left. We submitted a proposal to the Kresge Foundation for a half million dollar challenge grant, which I think we have a good chance of getting, and then our campaign goal will have a $15 million goal. This for an institution that never raised more than $1.3 million in any single campaign in its entire history.

Now there are a lot of things that go with that. The faculty is a lot larger than in 1988, and instead of 12 percent with terminal degrees, we are now 35 percent terminally degreed. We are beginning to increase enrollment. In the years when our enrollment dropped - and our biggest problem as a single sex institution was uneven enrollment, up one year, down the next, up and again down - it was a struggle. We did all the right things. By next summer, we will have spent $20 million on the campus. This campus looks like it has been totally rebuilt. Does it still have cosmetic needs, sure, but it is totally rebuilt with no deferred maintenance. We have a brand new academic curriculum with no similarity to the old one. Only one of our programs today looks the way it did in 1988.

You go through all of these changes, and you are frustrated about why your numbers don't go up. That's what was behind this co-education move.

We had made a strong commitment to being a single-sex institution. I had spent most of my career in women's colleges - I taught at Wellesley - my wife's from there and she is a product of a small women's college in Chambersburg, Pennsylvania - I was at Regis College, a Catholic women's college, for six years - Endicott College at the time was a women's college. When I came here I was very committed even though I have no daughters. I believed intensely in the benefits of a women's college and still do. But, I am a full-blown realist. When we tried and made all these changes, every year we would say, 'Why isn't it getting any better?' The Dean of Enrollment Management (now Vice President) said we can't compete, we are the most expensive private two-year college in the country. We can't compete when the place looks like a dump. We are new at this, and we don't have that, our technology is behind - now it is ahead. Why aren't we ahead of our competitors? Why can't we get our numbers up? No athletic program so build an athletic faciltity.

The final answer was we had become outmoded, we were being outgunned by the competition. So, I wrote a white paper for the Board indicating that we had done all these things over time, there had been a plan, some of it in the back of my head, had discussed it with trustees, and we knew where we were going, but we still hadn't turned the corner toward a goal of a thousand students. That had been our strategic vision, and mine since I came here. We actually put it on paper in 1996 as part of the five-year goal to be reached by the sesquicentennial. And here we are faulting, falling backwards. We need to get at least 240 to 250 freshmen; last year we had 176, the year before that 205. We are going to increase our discounting by a large amount, putting $1 million or more into financial aid. But, because it means we get less net revenue per student, we need more students

I worked that all out, six or seven pages singled spaced, made some charts, and said that to be successful, we must reach this enrollment target and, if we don't reach it, we must seriously look at co-education. They bought into the concept, but we came in at 206 freshmen, not 240, even though that was thirty more than the year before. We didn't hit the target, so I said we have to go coed. It was the only time in eleven and half years that we had a falling out. I started with the Board's Executive

Committee, which went ballistic - we had three meetings in a single month, each worse than the other. They argued that they had been won over to a single sex institution and loved it, think we are doing a great job, and that with a new curriculum, called connected learning, we needed more time. They said I was acting precipitously. I said no and that we are going to have deficits - I do financial modeling, having done them since I went to Regis. It is complicated, 150 variable interactive planning model, which I update regularly on the computer. So I updated it and showed them what would happen if we remained single sex and had big deficits. I got their attention.

The long and short of it is that because it is a wonderful Board - and that is one of the other things that has changed a lot, the Board composition - the Board said, 'Fine.' While we did agree to that, we are not ready, the alumnae are not ready, you have to give it more time. We can't vote for co-education in June. I said that is when our marketing begins. Well, tough, you have to have a committee, you have to talk to people, you have to reach out, you have to dialogue, and then we can make the move.

So, I set up a committee on co-education, four trustees, four faculty, and four staff - all of the trustees were alumnae, everyone of them hostile to the idea of co-education. Three of the faculty were hostile, but most of the staff supported the idea. We did discovery, we had looked at colleges that had gone co-ed and those that hadn't - all kinds of analyses - the future of single sex institutions, and so on. By the time it was all over, it was a twelve to zero for co-education.

I took it to the Board and said let's vote, We had television cameras here on this tiny campus - all over the place. Every channel was here. They were all interested in the story - it must have been a slow news day. They wanted to tape the debate, but I said you may not. In the cafeteria, students had been picketing one way or the other- one day they were picketing 'Power for Women' and 'We Don't Want Men,' and the next day it was the counter picketing crowd of women who did want men on campus. It was an interesting emotional experience. The Board voted unanimously. The Chairman came out to make the announcement; there was a lot of television coverage that night, and that year ended with the highest annual giving ever.

I pushed it earlier than any other college I know would have done. We were at the top of our game fiscally, and we were picking up our freshman enrollment. My feeling was, and still is, and I have never regretted it, certainly in the light of what has happened in the last two years, that you make these moves while you are strong. Most colleges, like Colby-Sawyer, that have really turned it around, waited literally until they had a foot in the grave before they made the decision. Since I know the VP and the former VP quite well, I knew that they had a $4 million endowment; they spent a million of it hoping to turn it around. When they were down to their last million, they went co-ed. I didn't want to go down that road. I said we know we are going to have to go co-ed in the next ten years, so what is the point of waiting?

There are colleges I won't name that are still in the same pickle. They run huge deficits each year, but they have large endowments, so as long as the market is generous to them, they can balance the budget from capital appreciation. But, sooner or later that run is going to end. So, if you know you are not going to make it, why wait until you spend it all? Why not do it while you are strong? That's what made it harder initially, but ultimately it was the right thing to do. We went co-ed on the top of our fiscal game, on top of our academic game.

Now we have taken on a project that is five times its size in fiscal implications. I had a vision that we need to be a leader in something, that we needed to find something other than the education field. There are a couple of schools in Boston that already have that. Keep in mind that we are one of sixty-four or sixty-eight institutions in the Boston area - it's a college town. And, so you can't be like everybody else. So the Village, which is now under construction, will be the first in the nation as a living-learning community, a continuing life-care community of which there are a couple thousand now. But, this is the only one in which life-long learning is a mandatory requirement for residents as long as they are mentally and physically able, unless we get a doctor's certificate exempting them. It's a very nation-wide market, so as a result we have received publicity in every major newspaper in the country. Whenever an article about innovation for the aging is written, Lasell College is mentioned. Our trustees feel proud; but just wait until it opens. The Village is under construction on a $56 million bond issue, and we are eighty percent presold. Eighty percent of the registrants are highly educated. I think this is the wave of the future. People don't want to retire and play cards, drink, and watch television. They want to be engaged. The next generation will have an even higher percentage of retirees with college degrees who are not going to want to retire to do nothing. We are going to build a graduate program in the Village as soon as it opens.

It is those kinds of initiatives, and there have been many smaller ones. One of the things we have promoted is entrepreneurship within the community. People are free to experiment. As a result, we have a single-mothers program that was set up by faculty. We have an extraordinary center for public service with over 30 percent of the students participating, again created by faculty. We have had a summer camp for HIV-infected young children for several years, supported by donations, again set up by faculty. In the connected learning curriculum, the head of the fashion program, who is well known in the area, has made inroads in Boston by getting to know the fashion designers; as a result, twelve of them now take our students on eighteen month internships. These really aren't internships, they are more like co-ops, only we do a four-year co-op degree instead of Northeastern's five-year. Our kids are in and out of the classroom constantly, instead of taking a year off. They work with designers from the inception of a line through to where do you sew it, where do you get the cloth, where do you get the buttons, how do you put it together, how do you market, and what is the profit margin. Pretty impressive stuff. These kids have jobs long before they graduate.

All these things are driven not by an individual but by a community. We really foster that. It means we make mistakes. It means we have to swallow hard sometimes. We've made some doozies. But, it you don't risk, you won't get a return.

Since going co-ed, new student enrollment went from 206 to 280 freshmen the first year and to 320 in the second. There have been growing pains for sure. Men were brought in as freshman, nearly ninety-nine percent of them. We did it by copying other places and setting up an athletic program. All the coaches hired for the men's teams were under strict orders, as was the admissions department, that we would not recruit athletes who couldn't make it academically. That has been very helpful. We have mandatory study halls for athletes who aren't making it. As a result, it has raised the intellectual climate on the campus, the kids are more serious. On the weekends, it used to be that no one was here, now they are going to a ball game or some other event. There is a sense of enthusiasm.

We are turning an old ballroom building into a high-tech classroom with faculty offices. We are constantly building. What is gratifying from a fiscal point of view is that our total debt service, which tripled this year, along with our total capital budget is less than six percent of our operating budget.

The biggest transformation, and this is worth noting as I did for the Board two days ago, is that two years ago most of them wanted to keep the initial two-year degree on the theory that you can't abandon the old market while you are building a new one. We abandoned the two-year degree slowly. Students got their associate degree and left because they could transfer elsewhere. Now they stay. All but two allied health programs - physical therapy assistant and occupational therapy assistant - are now four-year programs. There is no longer a two-year degree, so we expect an increase in the junior and senior population in the next two years.

[*Your role in developing the Board?*] Boards really do look to presidents to provide leadership and to mold it. I know they are supposed to be self-perpetuating, but it doesn't always work. What I learned in my role as a CFO sitting on two Boards and staffing them at Regis and Endicott is that they want no problems. Board members don't get paid to deal with problems, they get paid to revel in the success and to be proud of the institution, and that's why they give money. Who wants to give money to a dying concern? No one wants to be a member of a dying institution -

there are liability issues, you don't feel good about yourself, you begin to question your role as a trustee. So I knew I needed to turn the institution around before I could change the Board. I started this Village project and got people interested - the Vice President of Neiman Marcus came on board, corporate executives came on board, new alums we found who had not previously been interested but were now that we were going four-year because we were growing, we were building the Village.

As I said to the Chairperson on the Board - who had become Chairperson three months after I got here because at the time, it was a two-year cycle - she was an alum but had not held a professional position but was very committed, a strong volunteer - we have to do something about this Board. She said I know some people, and I will ask them if they will do us a favor. I said, Ruth, the day will come when people will be honored to be approached and asked, not whether you will do us a favor. And that is where we are today. I am not suggesting you pick and chose among the leaders, however.

I have also learned that getting very, very powerful and public figures is not the answer for small Boards because they have no time and are just lending their name. Usually, they are not even the big givers; the biggest givers tend to be your alums. Over time, we have brought people in who fit the profile of our programs - people in hotel management, retail world, a senior vice president of the Marriott Corporation, who has now gone off the Board.

I eliminated the sort of clique I inherited. In the first few weeks, I realized this wasn't a real board but three or four 'good old boys' who ran the place. All the women on the Board were 'also rans'; none of the real information was ever shared, financials were never shared, budgets were never shared. Now we spend our meetings talking about policy, and they all get monthly updates. They all feel empowered. Empowering is so important to Board development. They have to feel that they are really listened to and make a difference. I don't want to gild this conversation. However, the reality is that presidents run institutions, but if you establish a strong relationship of trust, particularly with the Chairman, that is critical.

I used to ask myself, when during the first few years I was furious about what a mess this place was, how could you get yourself into a mess like this? My wife reminded me if it weren't this place, it would be the next. Engaged boards know what kind of president is needed at a particular time.

This institution, because it had weaker boards in the past, lurched from problem to problem. They had appointed Arthur Griffin as president who had closed Grand Junior College. Why would you hire a president who had just closed a two-year, private college is beyond me. But, they did. When they were finally able to move him out into early retirement, they wanted somebody who was flamboyant and who made people feel good. That was Peter Mitchell, who was very good at what he did. But, he had no experience in taking an institution and turning it around. In his last year, they completed a comprehensive planning effort that was given to me. It had 21 Points. Point 21 was that if the first 20 failed, we should look at the possibility of selective four-year programs. I said we can throw the plan in the waste basket, we are only going to do Point 21, and that's it.

But, ultimately, the reason it works is the Board begins to have faith in its president, makes a dramatic change, and it succeeds. Then, it is open and honest. I think there are issues of stewardship involved. I don't play games. This is not for attribution, but for years I took no salary increase, simply to make it clear to people that I was not here for my own private gain, but rather open to sharing the success.

But, how do you get good people and keep them when you can't pay them enough unless you give them recognition for what they accomplish. Basic stuff. I am not a management guru, I don't even understand management. I'm a European Historian who had to retrain to stay in the same city as my wife. And, I ended up here. As I remind the Board constantly, fundraising for me is hard work. For my predecessor, it was the thing that made him tick. But, I do it. The big issue is what happens when Tom leaves? I said that when Tom leaves, a good Board will hire a good president who will not turn back the clock because he has seven people on the cabinet who will not let him turn it back. You've got to put in the infrastructure.

We are now going to have AGB evaluations of the president. We are going to have big evaluations, not just the Chairman of the Board and I. Why? Because I have nothing to lose. I love it and am secure here; they want me to stay until retirement and now make it financially attractive for me to do that. As a result, I can now introduce elements to the structure and the processes that when a new person comes they would be eliminated only at his or her peril. For example, I can't imagine the new president not having to do monthly reports. They are tedious, they take one to two days out of every month, and the news is not always good. And when it isn't good, I tell them anyway. It is better to tell the bad news because they are going to find out sooner or later anyway.

We are still a tiny institution, 99 percent of the world has never heard of us. When I came here I couldn't find the place. I asked a policeman and he said 'Lasell who?' I said to myself, we've got to change that. Now there is no question that they know we are in Newton because the Lasell Village project made us known state-wide. We were in the local papers - it was either BC [Boston College] or Lasell every week because we were fighting with the neighbors, there was picketing, and we were in the courts for six years all the way up to the Supreme Court. There was a landmark ruling that Lasell won hands down in Lasell vs. Newton.

We have had lots of visibility, and we are constantly fighting the neighbors because of our growth. No matter how nice we try to be, town-gown relations are tough most places, and they are really tough when you live cheek to jowl with your neighbors. There is a dormitory here and next door is a neighbor. Of course, the neighbor moved there knowing there was a dormitory next door, but once moved in they want the dormitory to go away. That is like living next to Logan Airport and then complaining about the noise. And, I am such a charmer, I used to meet with the neighbors and tell them right to their face. I don't do that anymore. We have an ombudsman, and she meets with the neighbors. I don't return phone calls, I don't talk with them. I am a red flag to them. It had some rough times for my kids with diatribes in the public schools when they were in public schools. My wife said she was glad she didn't have my name or she wouldn't be able to show herself in the neighborhood. It has had its ups and downs.

[*Your role in the bond issue for Lasell Village?*] Lasell Village, Inc. is a wholly owned, controlled subsidiary of Lasell College, and I am President of both, so technically I sign all the bond documents. Was I intimately involved? No. There is a long history, too long to ever tell - it's a book in itself. What made this so interesting is that we are a tiny college, and when the project was conceived, we had a $6 to $7 million operating budget. The operating budget for the Village won't be large, but its construction and development budget is $56.5 million. We initially did this on our own. There is a very circuitous route to all this, but once we spent almost $1.5 million of our tiny $3 or $4 million endowment, the Board said that's enough. It is credit to them that they were willing to do it; if truth be known, two of the Chairmen said they were doing this because of me. 'We know that's what keeps you here, and if that is what it takes to keep you, we'll do it. But there is a limit on how much money we are going to spend.'

Then we shopped for developers and finally found one with deep pockets who was willing to risk his own money for a return with a very handsome profit. They, combined with the Village, took a whole year to negotiate and develop complicated management agreements. They had already spent an additional $1.5 to $2 million on architectural renderings and early marketing because you have to sell sixty percent of the units you can go for a bond issue. So, we were selling smoke and mirrors because there was nothing constructed, there was an empty field. There was nothing there other than a hope and a prayer.

When we got to the bonding, I wasn't in there every day because the bond lawyers did most of that. They were successful in getting $40 million in short-term variable notes, all of it unsecured so obviously they wanted tight controls about what we can and cannot do. But, without the bond issue, we couldn't have gone forward. Now we are under construction with 80 percent of the units presold, and the first people will move in next April. The project is done in three phases because they start on one end with a total of fourteen buildings on the south campus; the north campus will be the last to be finished about June or July 2000.

The interesting thing is that there will be interaction with the College because it is right on the edge of the campus. There are already sixty of so villagers engaged because once you put your ten percent deposit down, you become a student. So, we already have them in our classes - the faculty is delighted, and our students love them. At first, they wondered who they were, but once they found out how interesting they are - and given that most of these people are highly educated as neurosurgeons, painters, sculptors, developers - they were fascinated. The other reason that it is so popular is that it is arguably the best location on the entire eastern seaboard from Miami all the way to Maine.

Usually, retirement communities are built in remote locations because they are the only places you can get zoning. What you end up doing is warehousing your elderly. They build beautiful mansions, what I call Naples hotels - gilded cages; but they are removed from everyday life. And, people die in them; it is a graceful way of dying. The people at Lasell Village are going to be alive because every day they are going to be interacting with students. Every building has a classroom, and you are required to do 450 hours of physical and mental exercise a year. There is a dean attached to it, and there will be faculty attached as well. And, we are a half-hour from Boston. It's perfect.

[*The transition from two- to four-year?*] That was a condition and part of my style, too. Rightly or wrongly, when I confronted the mess at Endicott - I could have gone back to Regis because they hadn't filled the position - I became much more assertive and took on a much more assertive management role of vice president for administration, and I basically ran the place. The president who was there was the first non-founding president, and she didn't survive a year after I came. Then, I broke in a trustee for a year, and then we finally got a new president, who is still there and is very good. I didn't want the job, and my wife wasn't about to move to Beverly and commute to Wellesley. It was there I learned you don't make hard decisions alone, you involve people to make tough decisions or you are never going to resolve problems.

So, when I interviewed here, having learned my lesson at Endicott by not having asked what condition the school was in. Imagine going to Endicott and a week later getting a call from the bank saying we are not renewing your line of credit. My first question was, 'What line of credit?' 'Well, you are into us for $800,000.' So, when I was considering coming here, I asked for financial information, enrollment information, which, when I saw it, I said I can't believe what I'm reading. So, when I interviewed with the Board, I told them they didn't know how bad a shape they were in and, if it continued they would be going out of business and that they needed to change course.

.   It's a long anecdotal story because that was my style; I wouldn't have come otherwise. I didn't know what the possibilities were of going four-year, but I did know we could not possibly hang on for a dozen or more years, if that long, as a two-year college. For example, Aquinas College, which is a women's two-year Catholic college in Boston in two locations and with twice as many students as Lasell had in 1988, just closed. Then there is Trinity, a woman's college in Burlington, Vermont, for which I was on the accrediting team many years ago, so I knew it. It was highly rated, but just announced it was closing.

I also benefitted personally from being put on the Commission [Commission on Institutions of Higher Education of the New England Association of Schools and Colleges] for six years where I was sort of their financial representative. I took all the troubled colleges. So, I learned what to avoid, what the competition looked like, who was doing what to turn places around, and so on - all those subtle messages. It also increased my stature before I was on board. They never had a Lasell person as a Commissioner of the New England Association.

So, it was a lot of those things. But, when you read my more private annual report, you get a sense of how I manage, what I tell them, and the message is what is happening. We are not a secure institution even though a $12 million endowment is better than $3 million. But, we have debt, and we are enrollment driven. And, we don't compete against colleges we used to. I try to explain to my Board that there are four leagues out there - I am a football enthusiast, born in Germany, it's my tradition, and I used to play, never seriously and was never very good. But, the analogy fits that we are in the junior or fourth division, the lowest professional division in England as it is in Germany. The rules are usually that if you are one of the two top teams in a division, you move up one division, and the bottom two teams in the upper division drop down a division making it more difficult to recruit talent. I said we have just moved up to another division so that today our number one competitor is Northeastern University, not Becker College or Dean College, both two-year colleges. This is anecdotal, but we just lost a kid to Penn - why he applied here we don't know - Penn State, Ohio State, Michigan State, all four-year institutions, long established with graduate schools. So it is much tougher competition.

To the credit of the Board, at its meetings we usually talk about broader policy, but last year we talked about new choices resulting from our growing stability and prosperity. We can either begin to still take the same students we used to, and because we have many more applications, can either give them less aid and get weaker students or if we want a slightly stronger student we are going to have to give them more aid because we will be competing with bigger institutions that give more aid. The Board voted, without any question, to give more aid to slightly upgrade our academic profile. Now if we get up to a thousand SAT average, we will be thrilled, but we are not there yet. But, that is a testimony to the institution; instead of saying we will continue taking weaker students, we now require the SAT. We will be upgrading. We have sent a message to the community.

Would You Do It Again?

I don't know. This has been an ambivalent experience for me the past two years. Part of me has been saying, should I have left? Would I be willing to do this again if I were younger on a second time around, I don't know. It takes a lot out of you. I think going co-ed took years off my life because you have to have the courage to go forward, have to have foresight, and the guts. You can't defer to trustees. And, why should they? Trustees aren't paid for that sort of thing.

[Ed.Note:] Further on Lasell Village, June (2006) reported that as construction got underway, the developer was approaching bankruptcy, and Lasell bought the company and took on the project itself. Financial benefits for the College included a management fee of $500,000 a year from the community plus a total of $4 million in lease payments for the land. However, two years after Lasell Village opened in 2000, Moody's downgraded the College's bond rating to junk status. Although the College is not legally obligated to financially support the Village's operations or its debt, it is on College land. Also, Lasell Village was a wholly owned subsidiary of the College at the time. The College transferred ownership to a not-for-profit entity, Lasell Village, Inc. Moody's, however, still regards Lasell Village as too closely related to the College, so the junk bond rating remains. President deWitt admonished that the community's rocky beginning could serve as a lesson for other colleges.

Dr. Peggy A. Stock, Colby-Sawyer College

The Institution

Colby-Sawyer College, founded in 1837 in New London, New Hampshire, is an independent, non-profit, Baccalaureate General institution with an enrollment of about 9,500 students.

Founded as New London Academy, its first coeducational students were admitted in May 1838 under its first teacher and principal, Susan Colby, who later married James B. Colgate. In recognition of Susan Colby Colgate's role and that of her subsequent generations, the Academy was renamed Colby Academy. In 1928, Colby Academy became Colby Junior College for women under the leadership of H. Leslie Sawyer who served until 1955. In 1943, the College introduced baccalaureate programs. In honor of its first two presidents, the College was renamed Colby-Sawyer College in 1975. Returning to its original coeducational roots, the College began admitting both men and women in 1989.

The core of Colby-Sawyer's mission is a commitment to liberal studies as a foundation for lifelong learning. Through innovative and integrated professional programs, close interaction among faculty, staff, and students, and emphasis on the importance of internship as a component of its academic programs, students are challenged to participate in leadership activities and to define and pursue varied personal, educational, and career options.

Upon her appointment in 1986, Peggy A. Stock became the sixth, and first woman, president of the College. The longest in tenure, H. Leslie Sawyer served twenty-seven years. Her immediate predecessor, H. Nicholas Muller, III served for eight years. Stock served as President until 1995 after which she assumed the presidency of Westminster College (Utah) from which she retired in 2002.

Peggy A. Stock

Peggy Stock received a BS in Psychology from St. Lawrence University in 1957 and two degrees from the University of Kentucky, a MA in Counseling with certification to teach individuals with learning disabilities and behavioral problems in 1963 and a EdD in Counseling Psychology in 1979.

Prior to her career in higher education, Stock served in various positions both in education and psychology. She was special education teacher for the United Cerebral Palsy of the Bluegrass, Staff Psychologist at the University of Kentucky Medical Center, Clinical and Program Director for Children & Adolescent Services, Northern Kentucky Regional Community Mental Health Center, and President, Midwest Institute for Training and Education, a small but highly successful consulting firm.

Stock's higher education teaching and research experience began as Instructor and Research Assistant for the Department of Psychology and Department of Special Education at the University of Kentucky and progressed through positions at the University of Cincinnati and Thomas Moore College. As she became more involved with teaching and research at the university level, her inherent ability to raise money, lead, and problem-solve propelled her in the direction of administration and management. The latter began as Counseling Psychologist and Associate Professor at Montana State University, where she became Assistant Dean in the Office of Student Affairs and Services. She then was awarded the prestigious position of an American Council on Education Fellow, serving as Special Assistant to the President of the University of Hartford and moved progressively there as Executive Associate to the President, which included the management of the Development Office for a period of time, and then as Vice President for Administration.

Peggy Stock has served on the Boards of the National Council of Independent Colleges and Universities, American Association of Presidents of Independent Colleges and Universities, Salt Lake City Area Chamber of Commerce, Utah Power

Advisory Board, the BMW Board of North America, and numerous others. She also served on the Selection Committees for Rhodes Scholarships in New Hampshire and Utah. In addition to her teaching, marketing, and administrative experience, Stock is recognized as a very successful fundraiser and a dynamic and effective speaker and communicator as well as the author of several major publications including Preventative Intervention Strategies and Delinquent Youth and Families (LEAA Report, 1976) and (with E Kessler) Organizational Diagnosis in a Religious Congregation: A Survey (1972).

Peggy A. Stock was recognized as the Distinguished Alumna of St. Lawrence University in 1991.

Peggy Stock's comments that follow are a transcript of her interview on August 22, 2003 in her home in Royalton, Vermont. The questions that prompted her comments have either been omitted or are indicated within brackets.

The Situation and the Turnaround

I think I was like most presidents thinking you know a lot more than you really know when you open the door. There is a huge difference between making yourself ready to be a good president and fully understanding and then really understanding it. I took the position because I was in favor of women's colleges and had a lot of confidence in myself in terms of marketing. But, as I walked in the door with my husband, Bob, and looked at the budget, I knew there was a problem. At that moment, a tape came from the National Coalition for Women and Girls in Education that indicated that sixteen year old girls were not interested in women's colleges. It was so bad that Bob said, 'What have you gotten us into?'

There was so much to do there. They hadn't taken care of the campus, it was awful. There were actually holes in the carpets, yet they wondered why they weren't able to recruit anyone. The place was disheveled. I wouldn't send my daughter there.

And, that is the conversation I had with the Board before I accepted the job. I indicated it was their fault, that it was their responsibility, and that they shouldn't hire me unless they wanted a mover and shaker. I was going to push and nudge them and be a pain in the neck because they had an awful lot to do and that it rested on their shoulders because they hadn't made the decisions and taken the actions they needed to. I wasn't going to let them get away with it. But, they still hired me! I think you have to be you or it doesn't work.

The first week I was there, the Vice President told me we had a $625,000 deficit and only forty-four applications for the fall semester, and this was February. Everyone I saw at the reception was getting cross-eyed, and I asked, 'Is this what we do?' I felt I had to make an impact in the first ninety days. So, I got money from the Board, individual donations, and we fixed up the Administration Building so that when anyone walked in it would look different. I made mammoth physical changes - painting buildings, took care of the grounds, and so on. At the same time, I brought in some external consultants whom I trusted, including a space consultant from Cambridge. The faculty handbook was an atrocity - the President didn't have any power at all. Previous presidents gave tenure to everyone, including the Registrar.

I got there the first of February, and there was a huge snow and ice storm, but, I walked down Main Street. New London is a pristine and wonderful town, but I couldn't buy a bra there because it would soon be all over town - 'Do you know what size bra Peggy wears?' But, when I walked downtown and someone was kind enough to invite me for a cup of coffee, I soon knew nearly every single problem of the College. I learned who the people were who were alcoholics, who was involved in sexual harassment - I mean the townspeople just poured it out to me. The town fathers took me out during the early days and wished me luck but didn't think I had the courage to do it. They said the image of Colby-Sawyer was bad.

I had some very good people that I kept. But, there were others who were more interested in their place in town rather than in protecting the College. There is, as you know, that delicate leverage between town and gown. And there were some things I wish the Board hadn't done. For example, they sold a $750,000 golf course that is now one of the top at the same time the College had a Sports Management Program - they didn't make the connection that they had this program. They were going to use the money to build condos. This was done just before I came, and I asked about it. They said the town wouldn't like it, and I said, 'Quite frankly, who cares?' But, that wasn't the attitude among some of the vice presidents who were running for town offices. So I did make some administrative changes.

I surrounded myself with people who were not yes people. One was a woman, Jean Wyld, who was one of the smartest, most savvy administrators I have every worked with, and who is now Provost at Springfield College. We'd go home, and I swear I thought I would become an alcoholic as we thought, 'What are we going to do?'

I did meet with the faculty and staff and told them what I had found. Every time I opened my desk, I would say, 'Oh, my God! Oh my God!' The first six months, I bought out tenured faculty - the alcoholics. I had conversations with the sexual harassers, fired one and gave another a second chance. In the end, I had gotten rid of five or six tenured faculty out of twenty or thirty. But, everybody knew they were incompetent. I let them go with a sense of pride - they resigned. For the alcoholic, I said we will put you in treatment and pick up the tab. He said he didn't want that and that he liked drinking and wanted to be drunk. I asked what would make him happy, and he replied, '$10,000.' So, I wrote a check for $10,000.

It was after three years when I noted that even though we had changed all our publications that previously didn't go together, and that we had done all the things that could be done at a woman's college, the slight increase in enrollment was due to demographics, not anything Peggy Stock had done. I remember very clearly that I was at the inauguration for the President of Wells College, and I said to my Chair, whose daughters had gone to Wells, that if I were president here, I would take the college co-ed in a moment. He turned to me and said, 'Why don't you do that at Colby-Sawyer?' I thought he was absolutely right.

I spent the summer reading, collecting material, talked with the chair, and formed a small confidential task force (I mean it didn't get out) of faculty, trustees, and administrators to look at the issue. We brought in a president who had looked at the issues and gone co-ed and a president who had looked at the issue and stayed single sex. Arthur Kirk was the man and a terrific president of Keuka College, a single-sex college that had gone coeducational, and Mary Linda Armacost, President of Wilson College, a single-sex college that had decided not to go coeducational. Wheaton College had just gone co-ed, and the president gave me some good guidelines: never have more than thirty people together when you go out on road, don't be the first person up, and do this in a short period of time so it doesn't gain steam.

So I announced it and said we will have thirty days of discussion and debate. The hot-lines and letters all went out the same time to alums saying that in thirty days the Board would make a decision. The place went appropriately crazy - but not too crazy. Women took over the administration building and then cleaned up afterwards. We had to teach them how to take over a building. The Board voted - one person voted against it because she felt she should, but she knew that the right decision was the way the Board voted.

We had gotten ourselves financially more stable in that three year period. I changed the Board enormously - people not giving money. Time, talent, treasure. I said if we are going to do this, then the things that must follow very quickly: I must have an athletic director in year one. We had a very wealthy donor who gave me $3 million, some of which I used to hire consultants. We started a capital campaign to build for the future - I forget what the slogan was. The Board had made the decision. The faculty - I still don't understand faculty after twenty-five years - voted 95 percent against going co-ed. I said, 'You understand I appreciate your vote, but this is not your decision. It's the Board's decision.' They were just like every other group - if we could just recruit this woman from Tuscaloosa, Alabama, it would solve our problems. But, the stuff is very clear. If you showed any intelligent person this research, they would say, 'Colby-Sawyer should have gone co-ed fifteen years ago when Dartmouth did.' Because that was the relationship - too isolated. One third of the alumni said they didn't care, one third said go for it, and one third said it was not a good thing. We had only two donors who said they wouldn't give any more money, but they came back into the fold two years later.

Having the hot line was very helpful - people could call in. We also went on the road - the chair of the alumni board, who was a trustee and is now Chair of the Board of Trustees - and when we went someplace, we had no more than thirty people. We explained, and it helped. As they would try to stone me and beat me up, Ann would step forward and say, 'I am one of you. You need to know what is going on.'

In the end, we had one year of planning, which was very important, to look at housing. We built eight female athletic teams in one year and hired eight male coaches. The strategy was to get the men here we had to have athletics. In the first year, we got 38 percent men. I'm proud of that. We built this gorgeous athletic and recreation center that was terrific for recruitment and retention. We realigned our academic programs.

In that year of planning, we did three kinds of residence halls - every other floor and every other room with separate bathrooms - different wings with separate bathrooms - separate bathrooms worked out best. Students became friends.

Going co-ed was the salvation of the College. It was the hardest decision I ever made. In taking it to the Board, some thought I was a traitor as the first woman president of College. This was the history of women's colleges - headed by men until recently. My husband, Bob, helped me develop a philosophy that if I could look at myself in a mirror after making the best decision for the College, regardless of what might happen to me, I went ahead and did it. The decision wasn't popular, but it worked. And, there is nothing like success to breed success.

We stabilized enrollment, going from 300 to 800, balanced the budget, developed a rolling financial plan with median and maximum enrollment targets that proved to be on target. It is very tough as a women's college. When I was at the University of Hartford, I would do the same thing. It was a very rough time in the 80s and very tough times for a small woman's college - they were going under - they didn't give enough financial aid and clearly did not have the right admissions staff. You make an impression when they walk through the front door, and that impression is formed very fast. But, they hadn't paid any attention to that. So I was always looking at the front doors to make sure they were always very clean, that there were fresh flowers out. I meant it was just very important when parents bring their children.

We redid the dorms, put new carpet in. I may be the only college president who bought items at auctions because we didn't have a lot of money. I would go to rug auctions, getting there early to talk to the dealers to tell them what I was about and would you would help me pick out the rugs. I went to one about an hour from here and bought $10,000 worth of carpets. Bob said, 'What check are we using?' and I said, 'Our check.' He said, 'We don't have $10,000 in our account.' I replied, 'Maybe we don't today, but tomorrow we will.'

Carpeting gives a real feel to a place. I also feel that is something major is happening every year, people get the sense that the place is on the move. I said that if we were not building a building this year or renovating a building, we were in trouble. There was so much to do. The residences were very old, the bathrooms were terrible. We actually bought residence hall furniture from the Army at ten dollars a unit. We had a nursing program, and I flew with the head of the nursing department and the purchasing agent to a hospital in Rhode Island, and we came back with $70,000 worth of equipment for $7,000. People kept getting better equipment and other things - there were two computers when I came. Everyplace you looked there was a need. It was a case of strategically making decisions that would have the greatest impact on people. We did have a gorgeous library, and we immediately fixed it up because it was so visible, making sure that the door was the right door. I made sure that I was available - I met with every set of parents because it is a small college. And, it worked.

The hardest thing was changing the Board because people had been on it too long. These were bright people, but sometimes Board members leave their brains outside the meeting. But, the Board did begin to develop and take pride, and I felt I had their support, which I think is terribly important. We had an AGB [Association of Governing Boards of Colleges and Universities] retreat with an AGB consultant, and that helped the Board. We had some very good leadership on the Board. I had three Board chairs, and I got along very well with each of them, which I think is key. As you can see, my style is very direct and honest. I would tell them what was going on and ask their advice and used it sometimes and sometimes didn't. At a critical time in the College's history, I had a Board chair who had been a corporate CEO four or five times, and he was enormously helpful to me in helping me understand some of the dynamics as we were going through this change.

It was good to have someone to talk to because when I walked through the door, I didn't know whom I could trust, and I picked Jean Wyld and said to her, 'I had to pick someone to talk to or I would go crazy here, and you're the one.' And, we have been friends ever since. We did a lot of strategic planning over a bottle of scotch. We would talk all these people problems - the two alcoholics, and this wonderful guy who was chair of the music department, but they had only six students with six faculty. You didn't have to be a genius to figure out we had to get rid of it. She would walk faculty down to my office - we would kid about its being death row! I think that the people who left, except for that chair whom I did have to let go, that they had been treated fairly. It's not what you do but how you do it, to let people leave with a sense of dignity.

We eliminated programs, but we had a process. We brought in Robert Schoenberg, Dean of Undergraduate Education at the University of Maryland, who lead a process of looking at all the academic programs. I remember the chair and I met with all the faculty after we had gathered all this information. Faculty were involved in gathering all the data, but they weren't the final decision makers. I remember coming back here and calling a friend of mine who is a president of another college, and she said, 'How are you doing?' I said, 'Ain't been eaten.'

I reminded people that we couldn't do everything but that these are the things we will spend money on, these are the things we will focus on, these are the things that will slowly be phased out, these are the priorities. When it came budget time, people knew, and the money followed the plan and, thank God, it worked. I could have fallen flat on my face, but it did work, and people were very generous.

You know, building new buildings, showing a campus plan for the future, having winning athletics teams with an income has its effect. The critical difference was going from 500 to 700, but asked about a critical mass, I said between 750 and 1,000.

It was a very difficult job personally - loss of sleep, and I most likely had two drinks every night. It was very stressful and at the same time to see the place come around was very rewarding, People said I was more interested in buildings than in people, but we did study salaries and raised staff and faculty salaries, but there were some problems we couldn't solve. The trustees, in their ultimate wisdom, had given health benefits to retirees until they died, and there were more retirees than people still working at the College.

I brought Tom Emmet from Regis College to go through the faculty handbook and said to the faculty, 'This would be the toughest two days you will ever go through but you need to know that this is the contract you make, that you made. I didn't do it, you did. And now we need to figure where we want to go because this isn't going to work.'

I had a vice president for finance - and you know at small institutions, the vice president for finance and the president make all the major decisions. There were huge deficits that had to be brought under control.

The real question is why did I take the job? I was an ACE Fellow with Steve Trachtenberg and said I never wanted to be a president because the personal cost was too high. I was 48, and my husband said. 'You gotta do it. Otherwise you will always say, I could have done it.' Steve told me I was getting to be a pain and that I was ready. So, he would nominate me for places like Queens College because he was a city boy. But, I like small towns. ACE came out with a list of about twenty women when they were trying to push female presidents. We would see each other on a search and on every search the same group would be there. As you know, to prepare for a presidential interview if you are a finalist requires an enormous amount of work. I said I wasn't going to do it. Some of them were inside jobs. It just wasn't the right case. And for me in my second presidency, the defining issue was the Board. If the Board wasn't good, that was it.

So, I told Steve, no more, you are stuck with me. At an interview for a presidency, there was a very nice guy who sat in on the interview, never said a thing. At the end, he said, ' I'm not going to hire you even though you are the best qualified. You are ready to be a college president, but not here.' Steve then called the Provost at the University of Hartford, and they talked about this small college in a small town. And, it is a charming place, all buildings are Georgian, and I could see what it could be. I told them they had to know everything about me including the fact that I am Jewish. I came to the interview without any preparation - they called me on a Thursday, and I came on Saturday just to meet the Board. They asked my reaction, and I told them it was the worst kept college I had ever seen - it was a travesty, an embarrassment; there was so much to do. The town, however, was lovely. I was cocky. I was committed to women's colleges. I told myself that I would do it, but it was a lot to take on - a tremendous job. But, my desire to become a college president got in the way of good sound judgment. Some good luck and some rich people came along, and that was the saving grace.

The three Board chairs were very supportive when it came to making changes in Board membership, and not only that, when it came to making difficult decisions, they stood right next to me. That was very important to me. You know, to meet with academic department after academic department and tell them these are the decisions we have made about American Studies, this is what we will fund, and this is what we won't fund isn't easy. There were bounces along the way, but in a small college with thirty faculty, they are not going to make the decisions. But, the Board chairs were with me, and that was very important.

The other thing is that when I would come up with something like building a building, I would always go over it with them beforehand so they understood it. They were very smart and would point out different things. I think a college president can do most anything if she has the support of the Board. And, in a turnaround, you need that plus money, money, money.

When I came, the endowment was virtually non-existent. They had borrowed from it. To overcome the initial $600,000 deficit the first year, I froze salaries and made people go through their budgets. We didn't have a purchasing agent, so I hired one. I put money in development and admissions, and I let people know how I was approaching things for the first six months. Every department came in with their wish list. It wasn't that they didn't talk to me. I let six people go. There were strategic decisions that we made as well as increasing the annual fund. But, we had a five-year plan that rolled forward each year. It wasn't big, but the Board kept us on it.

As I said, success began to breed success. We increased the annual fund from $500,000 to $1 million, and that was all put into the budget. I am a good fundraiser, and while I was there I raised $35 million for that small place.

Going co-ed was clearly the right decision. I suppose my error was in not doing it sooner, but I didn't have the ability to do it any sooner. People would have said that I came with that agenda and didn't give it a chance. In going co-ed, we had one year of planning, but it took several years to get up to the 800 student enrollment. I came in 1986, we made the decision in 1988 and implemented it in 1989.

[*Why did you decide to leave?*] I decided to leave for two reasons. One is that it had been ten years - that's a long time. Although I hadn't run out of ideas, I had done all the things I wanted to get done. New London is the kind of town that people wanted to move to. For example, I had a director of HR [Human Resources] who was making $85,000 in industry; I offered to pay her $35,000, and yet she came. So, when

I made personnel changes, I was able to replace with much better people.

We had a business department that was teaching shorthand and typing. I brought the chair to my office - she had done a lot in increasing enrollment - and said that we were not a secretarial school, and that the program was going. I had her to lunch at my house, and she said she could fight me on this, and I replied that she certainly could but would lose. I then went on to say that I would much rather you work with me and fix the business department. I asked why she kept these people, and she replied that Pat was her best friend. Obviously. I said let's retool Pat or have her teach something else because she is not going to be teaching shorthand and typing. I said we are going to get computers, and, by the next semester, Pat was teaching keyboarding. We hired some people with good credentials and began to really build the department. The accrediting team couldn't believe it.

Once a friend walked over to my car and said he wanted to talk with me. He told me I was working too hard, that I had a life, the place was doing good, and is going to do good, so slow down. That was good advice because the job can become all consuming, which is why I couldn't sleep well. And, it was only a sixty-seven pace walk from my office to my house so it was the last thing I saw at night, and I didn't have time to decompress. I am sure that is why I would come in, sit down, and pour myself a drink. The town in those days was pretty intrusive, and they knew what time I went to bed and got up. In fact, someone called a chair's wife asking if she knew that her husband's car was parked in front of such and such a place. She said she didn't know that.

It was a difficult but wonderful experience because I was able to realize what I was good at and what I wasn't good at. It is nice to see the place rebuilding now and being so strong.

Would you do it again?

Very few individuals, even the faculty and board, understand the demands of the job.

From every benchmark, I was a very successful president – but at what cost? The position was 24/7 for years. I rarely slept through the night, and I was always thinking and worrying about the College, as were the rest of my senior officers. I wasn't alone, but I felt very lonely. If it weren't for my husband – yes, I had one and five children – I don't know if I would have been as successful as I was. I do believe that I was the right person for the position at the right time. Outgoing, driven, a natural fund-raiser, a bundle of endless energy, and a judge of good from bad, I relentlessly did the job. I rejected such phrases as 'We've tried it before.' and 'That will never work.' Although I had the courage to make difficult decisions, no one but my husband saw the anguish I went through. Throughout my tenure as President, my sense of humor and ability to separate the important from the unimportant sustained my commitment. In addition, I did not take myself too seriously and was able to laugh at myself. In the end, my answer to doing it all again would be 'Yes.' My husband, however, says a resounding 'No' – the cost of success was too great.

Dr. Jerry C. Lee, National University

The Institution

National University, founded in 1971 and located in La Jolla, California, is an independent, non-profit, Masters I institution with about 26,000 students. The University has regional centers in major metropolitan areas in California from Redding in the North to San Diego in the South with a total of some thirty learning centers.

The University was founded in response to the compelling need for new approaches to higher education. In particular, it was felt that higher education needed to become more accessible for an increasingly diverse student population. Educational leaders were urging that it be geared to life interests, designed for the mature student, geographically convenient, and a lifelong process. The University took these as its guiding principles.

As its stated mission, the University "...is dedicated to making lifelong learning opportunities accessible, challenging, and relevant to a diverse population of adult learners. Its aim is to facilitate educational access and academic excellence through innovative delivery systems and relevant programs that are learner-centered, success-oriented, and responsive to technology." Its central purpose is "...to promote continuous learning by offering a diversity of instructional approaches; by encouraging scholarship; by engaging in collaborative community service; and by empowering its constituents to become responsible citizens in an interdependent, pluralistic, global community."

The academic year is divided into four twelve-week quarters, each composed of three one-month classes. Classes are held on evenings and Saturdays.

Upon appointment in 1989, Jerry C. Lee became the second president. The longest in tenure, the founding president David Chigos, served seventeen years. Dr. Lee retired June, 2007 as President but assumed the title of Chancellor.

Jerry C. Lee

Jerry C. Lee received a BA in Business in 1963 from West Virginia Wesleyan, studied Industrial Relations at West Virginia University (1963-64), and received a MA (1974) and PhD (1977) in Higher Education from Virginia Polytechnic Institute and State University.

He served in Human Resources Administration, General Motors Corporation (1964-66); as Vice President for Administration, Commercial Credit Industrial Corporation (1967-71); and as Vice President for Administration and Business (1971-84) and President (1984-88), Gallaudet University.

Dr. Lee has numerous acknowledgments of his contributions, including the American Association of University Administrator's Eileen Tosney Award, the American Athletic Association of the Deaf Distinguished Service Award, and the Association for Multicultural Counseling and Development Presidential Award for Exemplary Service. He holds honorary degrees from Gallaudet University and National University. He has served as chair of accreditation teams for the Western Association of Schools and Colleges and held terms on the President's Commission of the National Collegiate Athletic Association, the Board of Directors of the American Association of University Administrators, and the American Council on Education's Commission on Women in Higher Education.

Jerry Lee's comments that follow are a transcript of his interview on October 17, 1999 in his office at National University. The questions that prompted his comments have either been omitted or are indicated within brackets.

The Situation and the Turnaround

When I got here, I was shocked. I had some knowledge about the University, but I wasn't familiar with its mission or the term 'adult learners' because I had come from a very traditional campus environment, Gallaudet College. But, I was excited about coming to San Diego because we had a young child, and I made a promise to my wife that we would not bring our child to a campus until he was somewhat older. That was the primary and only reason I resigned from Gallaudet; at his age of two, we didn't want to raise him on that campus. San Diego looked great, and the environment was terrific.

When I looked at the University, I was intrigued by what I thought the problems were and this new concept of adult learners. However, after a few weeks, I called my wife and said, 'Stop packing. You can't believe this place, it's unlike anything I have ever seen.' There was trouble with faculty governance and accreditation; we couldn't keep track of the standings of all the litigation, and the media were having a great time at the University's expense. Unfortunately, what they were finding was true. I looked at the accounting system and found that it wasn't one at all but rather a very foreign form of bookkeeping in which it was impossible to track payables and receivables. So, for a long time, I would stay there, sleeping on a couch in the President's office, which had a shower around the corner.

So, I started out one day at a time sorting things out. One of the first things I did was to go to Mills College [then the location of the Commission on Senior Colleges and Universities of the Western Association of Schools and Colleges (WASC)] and asked, 'If you are going to close us, it would save me a lot of wear and tear. But if you would really like us to survive, that is something else. Give me thirty days, and I will come back and tell you what I think I can achieve.' That started a very fine relationship with Steve Weiner [then Executive Director of the WASC Senior Commission] that continues to this day; he has been a consultant for us and has a project with us.

But, it was pretty frightening for a while. When I looked at the financials from a distance in Virginia, I thought this was a simple matter. I'll just go there and in a year turn the place around because the numbers do not justify the revenue. What I learned after being here just a few days was that the enrollment numbers were suspect. We had a $10 million deficit. And, then I read your report, Ed [Report of the WASC Visiting Team, which Kormondy chaired] and other materials and decided since I was here I would make the best of it. One thing led to another. I met with WASC officials and then went to Oakland and made a presentation to the Senior Commission. Thank goodness they said, 'We believe you.' That was the start.

I sold a piece of property, and that helped. We had to reduce staff; we had approximately 900 employees in June of 1989 and 17 faculty. Today we have 625 employees, 11,000 students, and an increase of about 150 percent in full-time faculty. This all happened with a little bit of good luck and a lot of help from really talented people. The media have been very kind to me.

It has turned out pretty well, but those first years were pretty frightening. In January of 1990, I couldn't make payroll for some employees, and that bothered me very much. I didn't pay myself and some of the vice presidents and deans, but I did pay faculty and staff. But, with its mission, the institution survived even in those troublesome years with the attitude that if we hang together, work together, and believe in the cause, many things can be overcome. We've done that. The $10 million deficit that you knew about when you did your report is now a quasi-endowment of $180 million. [Ed. Note: As of June, 2006, the endowment was $283 million.] We paid cash for this new building. Our faculty salaries are in the top five percent of California Carnegie II A institutions, the vice presidents are in the top five percent of the AICCU [Association of Independent California Colleges and Universities] rankings, and our staff are in the top five percent of the AICCU, five percent above the CUPA [College and University Professional Association] median.

This is all because of the mission that was established in 1971 - we haven't strayed from that. We may do things differently, but we are interested in quality, respect, rigor. As you know, it takes longer to improve quality than it takes to reduce debt. In the next ten years, we will continue to focus on the mission and try to outlive some of our reputation as we provide an important opportunity for the growing population that will choose National over other universities. Today our competition is the CSU [California State University System] system; ten years ago, the gap between our students and the CSUs was miles apart; today the CSU is basically where our students come from. Our students are very much mainstream just as you find on any CSU campus.

We have to keep our tuition within the reach of students. Among the twenty-five or so California Carnegie II A institutions, we are in the bottom five percent in terms of tuition. Students still complain about costs - I understand that, they are customers or clients. We also work hard to eliminate barriers to student success.

The demographics of California, a growing state, include a large number of non-traditional students. This is the majority of our student body, and 60 percent are women. Because they have had jobs and families and other college experience, they are very qualified to assess their experience here. We continue to annually get very high reviews from our students on surveys.

[*What strategies did you use with your creditors?*] The creditors were beginning to pull back on our credit at the time because our income was so low. I needed time to learn the institution and to make reductions in strategic ways rather than just cutting. I told the creditors who I was, what my background was, where I had come, and gave them names of people in the DC area. They asked what kind of promise I could make. So I calculated what I could pay and over what period of time. Although they had the power to close the institution, I didn't think they would close an institution that had served some 48,000 students with its very important mission. I said I thought we had done well, but that we could do even better. Without exception, they by and large accepted my plan as to how I would pay them. It wasn't a contract, it was just my word. And, we paid them. I believe they sensed that the institution should probably have been closed long ago, but by 1989 they believed the institution had too much to offer and should continue.

I had no connections here, having come from Virginia. I began talking to people about the University. They began to listen and helped me out, and it became a good story as opposed to a sad song. It took me two years, until 1991, to turn things around. Part of the financial turnaround was that we sold some University property to the Church of the Latter Day Saints for $4 million. I am still grateful to them.

Then I closed a lot of centers - Palm Springs, Emoryville, Oakland Military Base, Mission Viejo. We had a School of Aerospace with a dozen airplanes, all underinsured, and a School of Engineering without one lab. I closed them. Then everything was in a state of flux. But since then we have made great progress. Now we have faculty governance, policies and procedures, faculty senate, councils, and council chairs; we have an enormous set of policies and systems - in those days there were none. But, I also had a free hand to do what needed to be done.

The early days were marked by enormous suspicion because there had been so many rumors about the University. My wife and I got to the point of not telling people where we worked. I remember being in the local drug store and being accosted by a former student. My son, then three years old, had an armed guard protecting him on the way to kindergarten. A bullet came through my office window in Mission Valley - I thought it was just random, but the Police Department concluded that to make that shot from that angle, it was shot on purpose.

There was some pretty tough stuff in those early days reducing and eliminating positions. There was a lot of history here. But, today that is gone; a lot of those people are gone. Today there is a great sense of community and an enormous sense of pride - here's where we were, downtrodden. Now we have tremendous respect from people like Don Kennedy [former President of Stanford University] and Steve Weiner. This is all good for the folks here because they knew where we were and how far we have come and still have to go.

[*What about the major overturn in senior administration?*] When we had 900 employees, a lot of them were administrators; the problem was that there were way too many administrators, many of them weren't very good. There were vice presidents and chancellors and associate chancellors, provosts, and associate provosts. There were layers upon layers creating this huge infrastructure. We were deep in administrators and virtually no faculty. So as I closed schools and locations, all those administrators left. Then we started looking at second and third tiers of administrators and found that we had fourteen vice presidents for a university of 7,000 people. We had a dean of the library even though we didn't offer library science, deans of enrollment and of information, and each of them had directors, and the directors had associate directors - an enormous number of administrators. A lot of them left. Since then, we have had more turnovers in some areas than in others, but the average tenure of our directors is now about ten years; average tenure of deans and vice presidents is nearly eight years, with one vice president having been here for more than fourteen years.

When I came, we had no faculty governance. I began to talk with faculty about its importance and what it means. And, I talked about faculty rank - at that time everybody was a professor. It was an incredible experience to go through. So, we borrowed policy manuals from USC [University of Southern California], Gallaudet, and other places for faculty groups to develop policies and Bylaws. They debated what the criteria were for faculty rank. I have some great memories of those discussions; they have paid off.

[*Your role in reconstituting the Board?*] The Board was established but knew they were in trouble; they had a new president, and there were numerous lawsuits and financial turmoil. I knew it wasn't a university Board - nice people, well-intentioned people, but not a university Board. My strategy was a recommendation to expand the Board with three new slots, and I recruited those persons. Given the public criticism, the $10 million deficit, probation by WASC and CCTC [California Commission on Teacher Credentialing], I looked for people of credibility so the Board would be strong enough to withstand what I knew would be a difficult journey. These new members were able to help me to professionalize the Board. Some of the longer-term Board members began to feel uncomfortable and realized they were in a different league. The new members began to raise the Board to another level. So, by a gradual process the composition of the Board changed. They have stood with me through this time. Now after this ten years, the Board may go through another transition where we may expand and bring on new members. The Board has been very supportive, never engaged in micromanagement, and it has been very generous to me.

[*What about your competitiveness that you noted in the survey?*] I just had what they call an 'executive physical,' started at 7 AM and finished at 4PM - a lot of eye-opening stuff. They had two 'shrinks,' and I flunked that part of it! Seriously, we talked about the things I enjoy, my personality, and I commented that I have always enjoyed competition. As a youngster playing sports, I was always first, second, or fourth in school. I liked to compete. In college, I played all the sports I could, and even today I still play competitively in golf, pinochle, or hearts. I don't like to lose. I like to compete. I like to sell things. I like the thrill of taking on an assignment and seeing how well I can do with it. In this environment, the desire to compete against great odds helped me to decide to take the job.

There are institutions in which I would not be very effective - for example, I wouldn't be very effective in a public institution nor in a research university. But, there was a desire to prove something, to win something - in this case, redemption for a struggling institution that in my mind and heart clearly deserved to survive. History illustrates that I was right. What a wonderful and satisfying feeling today when I see we have 60,000 alums, many the first person in their family to receive a college degree. I know that not all of them out there are successful, but many of them are and are doing quite well. Last month, they honored the four top teachers of the year in San Diego County, three of them were ours, and three years ago, the teacher of the year was ours. That gives me a great sense of pride.

We have a project that supports victims of domestic violence. A few years ago, I was invited to the YWCA. The first room was a shocker - it was locked for security. Then I went upstairs and found these mothers with abrasions, children whose clothes didn't match and crying, asking where was their daddy, their dog. I thought to myself, we have a project here. We awarded twenty-five scholarships to victims of domestic abuse. We didn't chose the recipients. Knowing that not all victims would benefit from a college experience and that not every one could qualify, we went to the Y and sought their help in identifying potential students. Last year, the first person from that group, a mother of five, received her degree. She's going to be a teacher.

The outcome of this is that you start with a desire to do something different, to take on a tough assignment, and see if you can do it. That's where the itch, the juice comes from - that's being competitive.

If you set fewer agenda topics and expect higher standards, hire good faculty and good deans, provide good support services, and encourage them to achieve some pretty lofty goals, you will do it. Also we shifted the focus to how much students learn rather than how much faculty teach. I used that approach with very talented people, constantly reminding them that I would provide the financial part and make sure we are resource healthy.

[*Was there an Interim President between Chigos and you?*] When Chigos left, the Board got some very good advice, suggesting they not go to an immediate search but to hire a group of consultants to manage things. They did. Two of the consultants co-chaired the presidency, and they had other consultants in HR, accounting, and other areas. It was a large group of consultants running the University when I came. They were doing very well, but I invited them to leave very quickly because I knew I needed to be in charge.

[*Your role in the financial turnaround?*] Primarily, I focused much more on expense than on revenue. Although most of our colleagues focus on enrollment and revenue, the answer is not there; it lies in strict expense management - growth by substitution, cost control. That's where the hard decisions are - that's the critical area, not the revenue side. But the real secret to reaching financial stability is on the expense side, not the revenue side. And, that is what I did - closing down programs, eliminating positions, improving how we do things more efficiently and effectively. If you have an area you wanted to grow, you do so by substitution - give up this in order to get that. I put the University through that kind of a planning process.

Management requires a lot more thought than just eliminating departments.

You can reduce a department by twenty percent and not really eliminate the problem, you just make the survivors disabled. You have to look at what you want to achieve in the short-term and the long-term, look at what areas are up for negotiation or reduction or even elimination.

In the early days, I spent more time watching those financial sheets each day, each week, each month. We had this horrible system, a makeshift bookkeeping system. That's how we survived. I kept tracking the numbers, and I knew where we were. We were in turmoil. But, I had great support from the University people because they were very frightened; I had great support from the Board, WASC, and CCTC.

A controversial decision I made was to close the Law School. It was making money, but it was a troubled place; the bar pass rate was not very high. Having gone to law school at night when I was working for General Motors, I realized the costs of time after working all day and going to school at night. That takes a lot. I felt badly for our students. I assembled a group of judges, higher education law school professors, and a couple of lawyers I knew. They looked at the matter very carefully and agreed that we should either go for ABA accreditation, or at least try, or close the school. We closed it.

[*Did your experience at General Motors influence the way you acted as president?*] I think watching my father taught me a lot. I learned things at General Motors that have been invaluable to me. Their concept of intensity - very competitive. I learned a great deal there. But, more valuable was my father, who was a very successful businessman with his own company, and whom I admired very much. Watching how he approached problems when I was younger had more to do with my tenure here and at Gallaudet than my corporate experience.

Would You Do It Again?

Oh yeah. Absolutely. No hesitation. I'd do it over again. I wouldn't take on another assignment now because I am very happy here. My family is very happy here. The competition now comes in trying to beat my son in playing tennis and golf. But also there are still days here that get the juices going. I wouldn't want to do another turnaround at this stage, but I am glad I did it.

Dr. Robert E. Knott, Tusculum College

The Institution

Tusculum College, founded in 1794 and located in Greeneville, Tennessee, is a church-related (Presbyterian), Masters II institution with about 3,000 students. The College has three regional centers, with a number of sub-centers, that offer graduate and professional studies serving some 2,200 students; the residential campus has about 800 students.

Tusculum College's roots can be traced to the founding of Greeneville College in 1794, making it the twenty-eighth oldest institution in the United States, the oldest college in Tennessee, and the oldest co-educational college related to the Presbyterian Church (U.S.A.). Its roots also extend to Tusculum Academy, founded in 1818, whose name was changed to Tusculum College in 1844; during its history, it had the future seventeenth president of the United States, Andrew Johnson, as a trustee. In 1868, the two colleges consolidated as Greeneville and Tusculum College on what is now the Tusculum College campus. In 1912, the name was officially changed to Tusculum College.

The original purpose, as stated by its founders, both graduates of the College of New Jersey, now Princeton University, was to provide a liberal arts education for the soon-to-be civic leaders of the American frontier in East Tennessee. This was the same spirit of collective deliberation and pursuit of the civic arts that distinguished Cicero's academy, Tusculum having been the name of Cicero's villa south of Rome. That purpose continues today in a dedication to the cultivation of practical wisdom and development of graduates who are actively committed to responsible participation in the communities in which they live. A central aim of the College is to offer an education that provides the basis for continued spiritual, moral, and intellectual growth and to join that education with opportunities for professional training at both undergraduate and graduate levels. It cherishes the noblest ideals of the Judeo-Christian heritage and seeks to instill reverence for and commitment to these ideals.

For both the Residential College and the Graduate and Professional Studies Program, the College employs a Focused Calendar, each semester comprised of four blocks of three and a half weeks duration, a student taking one course per block. For baccalaureate students there is a set of required courses, the Commons Core Curriculum. In addition to satisfactory completion of course work, all students must demonstrate competency in different areas, nine for baccalaureate students (*e.g.,* writing, analytical reading, critical analysis) and five for Professional Studies students.

Upon appointment in 1989, Robert E. Knott became the thirty-second president, inclusive of four appointed to acting status. The longest in tenure, Samuel Witherspoon Doak, served twenty years (1844-1864). Knott's immediate predecessor, Earl R. Mezoff, served the College for ten years. Dr. Knott resigned in 1999 to become Chancellor at Mars Hill College, then as President of Catawba College from which he came to the Tusculum presidency. He is retiring in 2008.

Robert E. Knott

Robert Knott received a BS in Mathematics and Physics in 1962 and a MA in Religion and Philosophy in 1969 from Wake Forest University, Master of Divinity in 1965 from Southeastern University, and PhD in Philosophy and Higher Education in 1975 from SUNY- Buffalo.

He taught at Mars Hill College as Assistant Professor of Philosophy (1969-75) and Professor of Philosophy (1980-82). His administrative experience includes: Dean of the College, Arkansas College, 1975-77; Vice President for Academic Affairs, Gardner-Webb College, 1977-80; and Provost, Catawba College, 1982-89.

Robert Knott's comments that follow are a transcript of his interviews on October

8, 1999 and January 18, 2000 in the Niswonger Commons at Tusculum College. The questions that prompted his comments have either been omitted or are indicated within parentheses.

The Situation and the Turnaround

On our way to the interview in Johnson City [TN], where the Search Committee met with six or eight people and wanted to screen down to two or three to bring to campus, Brenda [his wife] and I drove through the College. We were really intrigued by the old campus and the history of the place, about which I had been reading. But, physically, the campus just looked tired. You could tell that not much attention had been given to external upkeep. We found very little grass around campus; it turned out that they had not wanted to have grass because, as we were told later, they would just have to mow it! Walkways had about a twelve inch border on either side that was dead; it had been sprayed with RoundUp so there would be no trimming time. And, as to deferred maintenance, you could see paint peeling on the buildings. All of that was primarily from lack of resources. But, there was charm.

When we were finally selected and arrived on campus, I found that the institution was actually worse off financially than I had realized. They had first contacted me in February and announced my appointment in late April. At that time, the Trustees indicated that as best they could tell, the budget would be balanced for that year. Given no president or development officer, I said I was glad that was going to happen. In the interim, the Board had hired Bill Moss, retired from Peat Marwick and a former business officer for many years at Berry College in Georgia. After my arrival, Bill told me he thought we had a several hundred thousand dollar problem; so, I told him to get it all together to see what we are dealing with. By mid-July, that problem was $1.6 million. It wasn't all from that year because he had cleaned up a lot of things on the books that had been there, including listed assets that the College didn't have. The endowment, which in 1965, when then President Rankin left, stood at $5.5 million, was down below a million. At that point we didn't have anywhere to go - we had borrowed everything we could borrow and suddenly had things to cover, including how to make payroll in thirty days.

With the help of Bill Moss and key Trustees from the Executive Committee, we invited the five Greeneville banks to meet with us. The lead person was Stan Puckett, a friend of the College. We offered them a five-year plan that had been put together in two weeks; it wasn't highly sophisticated, but it did have projected budgets and guesstimates on enrollment. We had no track record; we had nothing but promises that we would try to make it work. The College had had its ups and downs for many years, so I didn't know what response the bankers would make. But with Stan leading, they came up with a loan of $2 million of working capital at prime plus one over a three year period, each bank with a piece of the total.

With those funds, we began to renovate the buildings. Enrollment at that point was at a low of 200 on the mother campus and 330 in the working adult program. We invested probably $1 million on three campus reclamation projects - reopening Haynes Hall [a dormitory], renovating what is now Welty-Craig [another dormitory], and starting work on Virginia Hall [formerly a dormitory, then an administration building].

We went immediately into a capital campaign in the fall of 1990 against all the professional advice because we really hadn't gotten to know folks at all. We were going out and shaking hands and saying, 'Hi, I'm Bob Knott, this is John Mays, and can you help us?' I was just more than surprised and caught off guard by the willingness of people to respond, both in the community and among alumni. It probably resulted from a fear about losing the College, a galvanizing force. I know it was locally because several people said they suddenly realized what it would cost to bring a college here, and now we are about to lose the one we already have. Alumni support had shrunk to about 8 percent annually - they had lost confidence in the College, and we weren't contacting them on a regular basis and with consistent information.

At the time, the Board of Trustees had thirty possible slots, and only twenty-one were filled - with no expectations of the Board. In fact, the Chair of the Search Committee, Jerry McDowell, who became Chair of the Board the next year, was recruited by people who said, 'You don't want to be a trustee of Tusculum College, do you?' So, we created the Trusteeship Committee that drew up some minimal expectations, including financial, and we set about recruiting Trustees. Of the twenty-one, I think there were only four alumni, so we decided we needed to get the alumni much more active and involved. Also, whenever we found someone who had the capacity to be a major contributor, financial or otherwise, we were quick to invite them onto the Board.

We chose not to do a Board of Visitors or Advisors so we could focus on the Board of Trustees at that point, expanding it from thirty to forty-five, with three classes of fifteen each. In the year before I came, the Board collectively gave $48,000, but, in the last few years, the Board has been giving well over $400,000 annually. We saw the Board as the backbone because there is no other steady stream of financial support. State aid to private schools in Tennessee is not significant; the Presbyterian Church is not capable of offering major support. So, it was our Trustees, alumni, and local community. We were very fortunate in getting some key local people when they first moved into town to set up their businesses onto the Board. All of them brought resources.

In the meantime, we had to construct or rather reconstruct the academic program. What was here was a hodge-podge of programs that had resulted from going after the latest federal money that was out there for whatever. As you know, most of those programs are 'after the curve,' that is, after you finally get the money, the demand drops, and they're on to something else. So, what was left was a large number of courses with very small enrollments that were not going to be able to sustain themselves.

So, we planned for a year and adopted a new mission statement that focused on reclaiming the old traditions of the College - the civic republican and Christian heritage of education. The second year, the faculty set to work reconstructing the curriculum around a general education component called The Commons, a required service-learning piece, and the one-course at a time calendar. All of that was driven by the coming together around the mission statement. I felt we had to refocus our energies to reclaim our integrity and to make sure we were spending our resources in a focused direction.

Alumni began to come back. They expressed enthusiasm for the program. Alumni giving in the first five years went from 8 percent to over 30 percent, which is a good number, getting up toward the middle of private institutions in the country.

I guess the most significant event was that first capital campaign with a goal of $10 million, set unanimously by the Board. We reached that goal in a three-year period with gifts and pledges. After we reached it and celebrated, several members of the Board told me that they had voted for it and then walked out of the room saying, 'Good luck, I hope you guys can do it.' The College had not had a vigorous campaign for years; it had a small capital campaign in the early 1980s for $2.5 million, which was successful, but much of that came from counting federal grants under Title III, not truly money raised in a campaign. So there was no confidence that the College could do it, and that $10 million was overwhelming. But, they did it, and that brought a new sense of confidence to the Board. They began to take on a new ownership and new pride in the College, turning around within the next six months to start a new capital campaign. Of the $11 million raised in the $10 million campaign, the Trustees gave just under $6 million and then set the challenge of giving half of the new $20 million campaign, which was set first at $15 million and then raised to $20 million when good progress was made on the initial goal.

We have been very fortunate in having Sun Trust Bank take up where the other banks started. They have worked hard with us to find ways to keep financing what we were doing while we were out raising pledges. The Bank accepted our pledges as security or collateral while a number of other banks wouldn't have done that. This building, The Niswonger Commons, came through [Trustee] Scott

Niswonger's major lead gift, and it is in and not just a pledge. But, by no means does it take care of the whole building. So, the bond issue enabled us to build it while we were and are still out their raising the money. I haven't seen the figures late this fall, but my guess is, this campaign, with one more year to pay out, will reach $25 to $26 million.

Faculty initiated and proposed changing the entire curriculum and the calendar at one time. When we came, I made it very clear that we had to reconstruct the curriculum and to rethink it from the bottom up because we now have a chance to do just that. Prior to our arrival, and I keep saying 'our' because there really were four of us that came from other institutions - which I think is significant because we didn't have to spend time learning each other and how we reacted. We brought in a chief admissions officer, a chief development officer, an associate development officer, and myself. Both the admissions and development positions were open so we were able to hit the ground running just within days of getting here because we had worked together before arriving. The admissions officer and I had worked together for six years at Catawba College, and the development officer and I had been together off and on for fifteen years. I think it is important to say that because you know how difficult it is to bring in new people, adjust, and get expectations together.

The faculty started work on the curriculum, and that went well. Then they proposed a calendar change, which was sweeping, to one course at a time. I really had questions about taking on both of those at the same time because, I had been around long enough in higher education to know how difficult it is to do either one of those let alone both of them. But, they were so enthusiastic about it - it was theirs.

Under the previous administration, the faculty had not felt they had the latitude to take ownership of the program and curriculum. What I did was to get them started and then got out of their way, to let them develop some pride of ownership. They did. After a long weekend when I went up on the mountain and sat and thought, I came back and decided I would do more damage if I tried to block their changes, that they should go ahead and try it, even if they slipped up some along the way. So they took it on, and that really carried us for the first five or six years, the momentum that came from that sense of ownership.

That was contagious among the students, and it went out to prospective students so we saw nice turnarounds in the new classes of students and the number of students interested in the College. That distinction of one course at a time caught the attention of a lot of prospective students - some for the right and some for the wrong reasons.

I think now, at this stage, the faculty is in danger of wearing out over the block plan. We have put so much of our resources in getting the physical plant reclaimed and keeping the place operating. Our annual fund or gifts to operations annually is, in my judgment, still too large for an institution of Tusculum's size and that the College is too dependent on those gifts. It's a scramble to make it each year. But, that has meant we didn't have the resources to carve out sabbatical leave time and other leave time to give the faculty a break every now and then. The block plan is grinding. I have taught in it several times over these ten years, and it was demanding. It comes at you with three or four hours a day, every day, without let up, and you have it for a month. For me, I could teach that way for a month and then walk out and do something else. The faculty can't. Ideally, I think they should be teaching six blocks a year instead of seven, but that a financial issue when you start looking at your ratios. I think it's important that, in the next phase of development, the College find ways to give some relief to the faculty so the momentum won't be lost. They have done some recent changing and refining. They've grown as they've tried to administer and offer this program, grown in their understanding of what it takes.

The physical plant has been largely transformed from what it was. While we haven't addressed all of the deferred maintenance, we have addressed the bulk of it with this second capital campaign and the $2.5 million item that is in there with the banks for special projects that include some renovations, but mostly deferred maintenance. With the current year, we should have all the residence halls fully air-conditioned, refurnished, and rewired with computer access; not addressed is the administrative software, which is a sort of jigsaw puzzle right now. The pieces are all working, but there is some duplication of effort. We did that twice over the past ten years, and it is ready for another reworking.

I think the College has matured with its new program and new direction, and that is one of the reasons for making the decision to step aside and let someone else come. When I arrived, there wasn't much that wasn't broken. However, I don't think there will be anything I can point to and say that is it alright and leave it alone, let's get on with something else.

As you know, this administrative responsibility takes its toll. I know that I could have stayed on for a number of years and enjoyed it, sort of gone to sleep, and walked through it as long as we raised enough money to keep it going. But, that is not what the College needs now; rather, it needs someone who will give the bulk of his or her time to fundraising. I'm an academic by heart and enjoy working with students and faculty. I learned how to raise money and what you have to do to do that. But, my greatest satisfaction came from all that work we did early on with the curriculum, the calendar, and reconstructing the athletic program. I concluded it was time for someone to come with the satisfaction primarily from seeing that the resources were all in and what was going to be needed to sustain the institution.

As I said earlier, we had a $3.5 million operating deficit that was underwritten by the $5 million bond debt. We got the operating deficit removed in the first campaign, and we were able to raise enough to clear out the books so that our books began to look good to the bankers. We were able to get a significant part of the debt paid down and the rest of it rolled over to the bond issue. That is, we were able to cover the operating side of the deficit, which was about $1.8 million. Importantly, the endowment has gone from less than $1 million to about $10 million, which in a collateral sense, is underwriting the bond issue. With gifts and pledges, the campaign will probably bring in another $4 to $5 million. Two years down the road, the bond issue kicks in in terms of starting to pay back some principal. I think that is manageable over a fifteen to twenty year period, depending on how it is set up. All of the assets that have been raised will be in the endowment.

So, I think the College has a fighting chance - no, more than a fighting chance - it has an opportunity to go on and reclaim a heritage that was here years ago, namely its good name in the region. I have talked with a number of alumni who were back here for Homecoming last weekend; when they saw the new Niswonger Commons and the campus, their enthusiasm was just very, very high.

There has been a lot of satisfaction in this for me and Brenda, and it is better to leave town leading the parade than being run out on a rail.

[*What was your role in the curricular revision?*] In that first year, I thought my role was to work on developing a mission statement that was more than what appeared on a piece of paper. We had twenty-one full-time faculty at that time and probably fifty adjuncts who taught in the day and evening adult program. I invited the heart of the faculty, the twenty-one full-timers, to the President's house twice a month on Thursday afternoons. We met on the side porch, which was large enough to do it. There is now a legacy at Tusculum of 'Side Porch Meetings,' as they were called. They weren't meetings to make decisions, but rather to talk. I gave them a chance to tell me what they thought was needed and what they wanted to do. They . had major involvement in shaping the mission statement that the Board adopted. The Board led the eight committees involved in the strategic planning process, each committee chaired by a Board member. But, the faculty served on all those committees along with staff, alumni, students, and townspeople - anyone who wanted to be in the process - we had over a hundred people involved.

In those discussions on the side porch, the group started reading together some of Samuel Doak's material [Doak was one of the College's founders], Cicero's works, and a variety of other things as a stimulus to our thinking. My task, as I saw it, was to get the faculty focused on an approach to the programs that would be manageable and would be an outgrowth of the mission, as we were forming it. Then, my task was to step back and let the faculty take the lead in developing the curriculum and become, in some ways, a cheer leader for them, to compliment them when they had done something well and not jerk them around when I felt that things were not going they way they should.

The faculty were too fragile at that time - they didn't have a lot of confidence in themselves. In fact, one of the former Board members wrote me a letter before I came saying that if I fired the six senior faculty members the place would be in great shape. That was how harsh things had come between some of the Board members and the faculty. Yet, it was those six faculty members who took the lead in developing the new program. I tried to stay very close with them, spending time in meetings as they began to construct their curriculum. They were receptive to advice I would give because they had felt dispossessed in the past and did not feel that their thoughts were being taken seriously.

Further, there was even a fairly conscious move among officers of the Board to talk about discontinuing the residential college campus and offering only the professional studies program. Thus, when I came in with an emphasis on the residential college and started talking academic matters with the faculty, they developed a sense of ownership and of my investment in them that made them open to discussion and pursuing ideas. I think there was credibility because I had come out of the classroom - that proved helpful. The discussions really were very constructive and quite warm, without much friction or hostility.

Regarding reconstituting the athletic program, when I arrived, any money we had in scholarships was in athletic scholarships; there was nothing going to the general student body. Part of what we needed to do was to firm up that base since we were able to recruit in that way and then try to grow the non-athletics part of the student body to go along with it. At the time, we were in the Tennessee Virginia Athletic Conference, which was more of a scheduling convenience than a conference. So we looked for a conference to which we could belong that would be a true one in the sense of setting admissions expectations and performance standards, facilities review, and a commissioner who was at least part time to work with. We found an initial home in the Mid-South Conference and then two years later moved to the South Atlantic Conference, where the College is now. This was a move from NAIA to NCAA, Division Two, a move that put more restrictions on athletic scholarships than was the case under NAIA.

I felt the College had to be in a competitive conference where we had sufficient restrictions on athletic money to allow us to start moving resources as they grew over to the non-athletic side. When I left, about a third of the money was going into athletic scholarships, and two-thirds was being awarded on the basis of academic merit or need. All of that was part of establishing or re-establishing the public image and reputation of the College. Unfortunately, today, most of the College's reputation is athletics in the public mind. So what we did was to try to get the College linked to some reasonably well known and stable academic institutions through athletics. It took several years to get there, but I think it eventually got the College where it needed to be.

[*The bond issue?*] As I mentioned before, when I arrived we ended up with about a $3.5 million debt that was at an interest rate of prime plus one through five local banks, each of them having a piece of it. They had no reason to support us, but they did, even with a new administration with no track record. They stood behind us and helped us carry the debt. The problem was that it was a pretty stiff interest rate relative to what else was out there. Yet, the College was not strong enough financially to float its own bonds. So we made contact with several banks, Sun Trust being one of them, to talk about what it would take to get a letter of credit to underwrite our going to the public for the issuance of bonds, after they were approved, to help build educational facilities. Sun Trust Bank, of Knoxville, was one that stepped forward, indicating they would like to be part of the bond issue even though they were not part of the loan arrangement.

We went into negotiations with them, and they gave us a letter of credit with which the College underwrote the change of the $3.5 million debt into a $5 million bond issue. It had some construction money in it in addition to servicing the debt; it also dropped the interest rate from prime plus one to less than five percent. Then as the capital campaign took hold and pledges came in, we borrowed an additional $10 million, which increased the total debt to $15 million. But, we had pledges coming into the endowment or going towards construction that offset $5 million of the additional $10 million. All of that is at the less than five percent interest rate.

We arranged it so that we only paid the interest during the five-year phase of the campaign payout. In 2002, it rolls over into a long-term bond issue where we would begin paying on the principal along with the interest. By that time with all the payout in the campaign, there would actually be money that the College and the Bank will have to decide whether to pay down the bond or keep it in investments where we would earn more than we would be in paying interest on the bonds. In all likelihood, the money would stay in investments, using the growth to pay down the bond principal. Whereas the Greene County Bank and the other banks had really helped us at the outset to keep our doors open, it was Sun Trust that stepped up and really gave us much more sound financial footing.

[*Your role in reconstituting and developing the Board?*] Bruce Alton, of Academic Search Consulting Service, which had conducted the presidential search, left me and the Trustees a report in which he indicated seven or nine major points that the College needed to address. At or near the top was the need for reconstituting the Board with people who had a more deeply felt sense of ownership of the College. Also the Board had been recruited with no expectations, financial or otherwise. So we deliberately set out that first year to create a Trusteeship Committee and through it to establish a list of expectations of Trustees. It was a very conscious effort to rebuild the Board, to bring more alumni on.

I believe that reconstituting the Board was probably the backbone of generating the turnaround we accomplished. I thought it was my role, a major responsibility, to personally make the case to as many of the potentially new Trustees as I could and to sustain a relationship with the Board in which I tried to maintain their confidence in what we were doing.

Would You Do It Again?

In my professional career I don't know that I have had anything any more rewarding professionally and personally than seeing the College come back to its feet and regain stability and some momentum for the future; watching a Board go from being very tentative about what they could do and how they could lead to becoming quite confident, which was through the success of that first capital campaign; seeing a faculty go from being demoralized to having a real sense of commitment and spirit to what they believed and what they were doing with the curriculum and students; and watching a student body that didn't really have much pride in themselves and the College become one that came to really believe in themselves. That was all extremely rewarding to me, and I have not had another experience that was as rewarding as that. So would I do it again? Yes, knowing that it was out there as something to enjoy. Would I have taken it knowing all the financial strains and difficulties? Probably not.

Dr. Garry D. Hays, United States International University

The Institution

United States International University (USIU), founded in 1952 and located in San Diego, California, was an independent, non-profit, Doctoral Research/Intensive institution at the time of the interview (1999). Then, the University had off-campus sites in Irvine, California as well as in Nairobi and Mexico City with a total enrollment of 3,400, which included students from more than 90 countries; some 1,400 students were on the San Diego campus as is the case now.

The University was founded as California Western University and was located in Point Loma, on what is now the campus of Point Loma Nazarene University. In the late 1960s, the name was changed to its present version to reflect a commitment to international education. USIU was one of the first universities to embrace the concept of multicultural, multinational education. A federal government land grant in 1965 enabled the University to acquire its present 160 acre campus in Scripps Ranch, previously the U. S. Marine Corps' Camp Elliott. Construction on what was known as the "Elliott Campus" began in 1968, and programs were offered at both the Point Loma and Scripps Ranch sites until the sale of the Point Loma campus in 1973.

The mission of the University is "...to promote the discovery and application of knowledge, the acquisition of skills, and the development of intellect and character in a manner which prepares students to contribute effectively and ethically as citizens of a changing and increasingly technological world." The mission is "...carried out in an environment which encourages intellectual and scholarly development; fosters an openness to a wide range of ideas, cultures, and people; and enhances personal growth." The mission is achieved through its programs of study resulting in the following outcomes: higher order thinking, literacy, global understanding and multicultural perspective, preparedness for career, and community service.

The academic year was divided into five terms: four quarters, each eleven weeks in duration with a three-week intensive study session between the fall and winter quarters.

Upon appointment in 1992, Garry Hays became the second permanent president, replacing an acting president. The founding president, William Rust, served thirty-seven years in that capacity. Dr. Hays retired at the end of June 2001. Shortly thereafter USIU merged with the former California School of Professional Psychology, which had been reorganized and renamed Alliant University. Alliant International University-San Diego is the name of the merged institution.

Garry D. Hays

Garry D. Hays received a BA in History in 1957 from Southwestern College (KS) and a MA in 1959 and PhD in 1964, also in History, from the University of Kansas. He taught history at Southwestern College full-time (1960-63; 1964-66) and as a teaching assistant (1963-64).

He served as Assistant Vice President for Academic Affairs at St. Cloud State University (MN) (1966-68); Dean of the College at Virginia Wesleyan College (1968-70); and Director of Academic Planning (1970-71), Vice Chancellor for Academic Affairs (1971-76), and Chancellor (1976-82) of the Minnesota State University System.

From 1982 until his appointment at United States International University, he served in various executive positions with the HELP group, which is comprised of several interrelated, private, non-profit corporations created to assist students in gaining access to postsecondary education, including: President of the Higher Education Assistance Foundation, then the largest guarantor of student loans (1982-90); Chairman of the Board and Chief Executive Officer of the Higher Education Loan Programs of Kansas, Washington, D.C., and West Virginia (1982-92); and Vice Chairman of Help Management Corporation, the parent organization of the various corporations in the HELP group (1990-92).

He has served as First Vice Chair of the San Diego World Affairs Council, Honorary Director of the Japan Society of San Diego and Tijuana, a member of the Task Force on Teaching Effectiveness and Student Learning of the Western Association of Schools and Colleges, Chair of the Greater San Diego Chamber of Commerce's International Trade Development Coalition, and member of the Chamber's Public Policy Committee, among others. He was recognized by the Scripps Ranch Civic Association (1993 and 1994), received the Leadership Alliance's Professional of the Year Award (1995), and named 1997 "Headliner of the Year" for higher education by the Press Club of San Diego.

Garry Hays' comments that follow are a transcript of his interview on October 17, 1999 in the President's office at United States International University. The questions that prompted his comments have either been omitted or are indicated within brackets.

The Situation and the Turnaround

Fortunately, when I got here there were not a lot of surprises because the Board Committee members that I had talked with before coming out had been wonderfully candid as had been the Acting President. I had heard of USIU only one time before they contacted me, and that was when the hockey coach at the University of Minnesota was fired. I was then living in Minnesota. A month or so after the firing, I read in the *Minneapolis Tribune* that he was going to United States International University to start a hockey program. My reaction, 'Hockey in San Diego?' That was a number of years ago, and I had forgotten all about it.

One day in 1992, I was sitting in my office in St. Paul, I got a call from Ginny Lester, who at one time had been president of Mary Baldwin College in Virginia. Ginny and I had served together on the Commission on Women in Higher Education of the American Council on Education. Ginny had gone on to other things and, at the time, was working for the Association of Governing Board's presidential search service, when they still had one. She called me to say she was staffing the Board of USIU in San Diego, which was trying to find a president. She added that, by the way, they are $28 million in debt and in Chapter 11 bankruptcy, but could she put my name in. I said, 'Ginny, why would I do that?' And she said, 'Well, will you just come out and talk with a committee of the Board?' So I said I would and thought that I would just come out and talk with the Board and that would be that.

But, I began to get intrigued - it was an horrendous mess, obviously - by first, the challenge of taking on a place like that and turning it around, and second, the challenge of seeing if we could do something significant in the area of multicultural, multinational education. At least, there was a mind set toward that end particularly among the faculty. They had screwed it up pretty badly because the founding president's vision of international education was simply to have campuses all over the world. When I came here, I asked the question, 'What is international about this place?' The answer was always that we have a campus in Kenya, and one in Mexico City, and one in London, which I have since closed. I said I understand where the campuses are but let me ask the question again: 'What has that got to do with what's going on in the educational process?' The answer at that time was, nothing. But, at least there was a mind set. So, I got intrigued as to whether we could do it or not.

After the Board offered me the job, I came back twice more because while I was willing to take a risk, I didn't want to preside over a funeral. I wanted to have some sense that I could do it. But, in that process of coming back, talking with the Board and the Acting President, Kenneth McLennan, I pretty much knew there would be very few surprises when I got here.

The Acting President had stopped the bleeding. There was no more debt incurred after 1990; all the debt, $28 million, had been incurred prior to that time. Bill Rust, the founding President, had been here thirty-seven years and had created great damage in the community. His reputation and that of the University was absolutely at rock bottom. So, a big task in coming in was not only what needed to be done on the campus but also to change the image within the broader community so people would know there was different leadership and a different set of values than previously.

So, what I knew when I came in was the existence of the debt even though there had been no more debt incurred. Also there was still a very top-heavy administration. I inherited nine vice-presidents and eight deans for a little place like this. The Acting President had done a great favor in that he abolished an inflated athletic program that had twelve NCAA Division I athletic teams! They were playing the big kids, or trying to. They were spending literally millions of dollars but bringing in very little revenue. So, he had abolished that program.

And, he had started to repair the relationship with WASC [Western Association of Schools and Colleges]. His name is Ken McLennan, a retired Marine General, an incredible human being. He had repaired credibility with Steve Weiner and Ralph Wolff [then, respectively, Executive Director and Associate Executive Director of the WASC Commission on Senior Colleges and Universities]; that had been a real problem during the Rust presidency. It was the Visiting Team in 1989, chaired by Paul Locatelli [then and still President of Santa Clara University, CA], that really saved this University. Steve asked me once to give a paper at a WASC Annual Meeting about the role of accreditation with an institution that had this kind of problem. I said that this institution would be gone if that 1989 team had not done what it did.

In that visit, they discovered an international campus that Rust had never told the Commission about. As a result, institutional integrity was absolutely non-existent. Ken had started to repair that by being fully candid in dealing with the problems. But still, there was a lot to be done. The institution was still on probation when I came. Although Ken's credibility was still strong with Steve [Weiner], he didn't know me from Adam, so it was a matter of making sure that the way we dealt with the Commission was open and candid. Particularly in the early years, we spent a lot of time making sure that Steve knew exactly what we were doing. But, the probation was a major issue.

Academically, everything needed to be done. One of the first things I did was to bring in consultants in each of the academic areas in which we had programs. We eliminated some weak programs; for example, they were trying to do electrical engineering with inadequate faculty, inadequate equipment, so we eliminated the program. They were offering the PhD in Psychology as well as the PsyD; however, most of the students in the program were practitioners and did not want to be researchers or college professors. They were mental health workers working on a doctorate while working in a clinic. With few exceptions, while most of the faculty in psychology at that time had doctorates, they were not researchers. So, we had a student body and faculty geared for a practitioner program, but most of the students were in the PhD program. So we stopped admission to the PhD program in 1993.

We had a program in Education that was a money maker with 150 students, but, it was a joke. It was a touchy-feely kind of program. The Education Department had very little to do with it. The founding president had created a whole separate group to run that program. It had no academic standards. We closed it even though it meant losing those 150 students.

So, we closed some programs and changed others. I submitted a three-year academic plan to WASC in December 1993 that laid out where this institution was going to go academically. Incidentally, about a third of the faculty are new since 1993.

The kinds of things we had to do, we did; we wanted to get rid of the debt. We had to cut the payroll. I kept one of the nine vice presidents, and he is still with me - he had been hired by Ken McClennan. He is a finance guy, so he has been part of the solution rather than part of the problem. He was a partner with Peat-Marwick here in town.

We reorganized from eight little fiefdoms, the schools, each with a dean, into two colleges - a College of Arts and Sciences and a College of Business. That cut about a million dollars annually out of the payroll. I came at the end of May, and we implemented that change in the middle of July. I brought in a new senior management group, except for the VP for Finance. As I said earlier, we evaluated all the curricular programs and made changes there. We got the debt behind us in October 1993.

When I arrived, I found a campus that was in a total state of disrepair. All the roofs leaked - even with the small amount of rain we get in Southern California. The deferred maintenance was huge. Technology was non-existent - even the library had no technology. The software record system was a proprietary one that had been created by an employee who had retired but whose son was holding the institution hostage because he was the only one who knew how to hold it together. So, we laid a fibre-optic system, put in a new telecommunications system, a new software information system - one of the standard packages - wired the dormitories, developed computer labs, and built the library with the technology that needed to be there. That was a huge void. The deferred maintenance was really something. So, we started out by remodeling faculty offices.

The first year, my wife and I started having receptions for faculty and spouses at the beginning of the term. The first year, in spite of the debt and being in Chapter 11, there was still an upbeat feeling among the faculty and staff - at least there was a new president, and there was some hope. By the second year, we had gotten out of debt and Chapter 11 - that was a pretty good experience to start the academic year. By the third year, we had remodeled the faculty offices, so the big topic at the reception was about who had the best office. The Education people said theirs were the best on campus, and the Arts people said theirs were. I told my wife that if we could keep them arguing about who has the best office, we were OK. And, that is probably indicative of another major problem I had - that was morale.

Rust was an absolute dictator - authoritarian, managing by whim. Faculty told me stories about how they wouldn't know whether on one day if he met them on campus he would be nice to them or fire them. I've used the metaphor of the abused wife syndrome. There was a victimized quality.

There were some good faculty - I did not find a terrible faculty. We had good folks who suffered all those years - I am amazed they stayed. It wasn't the case that only those who stayed were those who couldn't get jobs elsewhere. That says something about the spirit of this place and a vision of what this place could be, a real international institution. That's what kept them going as well as the diversity in the student body and their classes. But, they were beaten down. So, what happened is that most of the faculty would teach their classes but had otherwise withdrawn from the University. One of the challenges early on was to get the faculty involved again in the University, more than just teaching their classes. We worked pretty hard on that and still do. That was another major challenge to begin with.

Ken McLennan had started that process. There had been no faculty senate here; he started a faculty senate and developed with the faculty a constitution for shared governance. All through that two and a half year period he was here, he was often uncertain whether he could meet payroll or whether the University was even going to be here. But, he would hold open forums weekly with the faculty to keep them up to date and involved. That was beginning to change before I got here. There was a need to continue that interaction with the faculty, assuring them that they were going to be involved. The point of this is that the renovation of the faculty offices was a small but symbolic way of beginning to send messages to them.

This building had burned sometime in the late 80s, and although it is the first building one sees on coming onto the campus, they had left it looking like a bomb hit it, from the pictures I have seen. When Ken came as Acting President, he realized that the outside of it had to be fixed up, but he didn't want to spend the money to fix up the inside. They fixed up the outside so it didn't look as if a bomb had hit it. The President's Office was across the way. When I came, I left it pretty much as it was - pretty beat up furniture, not a very attractive office. My Board members would come and say 'This is terrible, you've got to fix up this office.' But, I just left it that way. We fixed up the classrooms and the faculty offices. I just stayed here until I got a petition from the faculty senate and staff council saying please fix up the office. So, in year three, we finished the inside of this building. There were many things like that as evidence of how bad the morale of faculty and staff was and how little it took to turn it around.

There was a need for a cultural change with the staff as well because they too had been so beaten down, and the future was so uncertain. Particularly at the staff level, there was a kind of 'cover your ass' mentality. One of the things I found was that departments did not talk to each other, so I began talking about the ripple effect. Every time I met with staff, I reminded them that every time they make a decision in their area, it affects not just theirs; there is a ripple effect throughout the University. One of the things I feel very good about is that there is now within the staff a sense of we are in this for the University, not that we are in this for the Admissions Department or the Financial Aid Department or whatever.

The external relations - that was a huge thing. McLennan had not done much to improve external relations and had not tried because he had his hands full internally. The external turnaround with regard to image, visibility, and involvement all remained to be done. But, there again, the community was open to somebody who would be candid with them and who had integrity. Rust, justifiably, had a reputation of being a wheeler-dealer - somebody here in town told me he should have been in real estate instead of higher education!

I dealt with him for about eight months relating to the then London campus. He had created what, under British law, was called a charitable trust, which was a legal, non-profit entity that permitted a foreign university to do business in England without adverse tax implications. He had created a separate Board over there for the trust, and he was chair of the Board. A couple of his henchmen or cronies were on the Board. In 1981, Rust caused his Executive Vice President here to write a letter to him in his capacity as chair of that charitable trust saying that it was not the intent of USIU to terminate the lease to IUE Ltd, which was the name of the trust, on the Bushy campus until the year 2021. When Rust was finally ousted and was no longer

President, we started talking about the London campus, and he started waving this piece of paper saying 'No no, that as chair of the Board, the Board of the charitable trust controlled the London campus.' I tried to negotiate with him for about six months and realized that was going nowhere. So, we brought suit against him in British court in 1992; we finally won, but it took us until April 1994, during which time under British law, we could not occupy the campus. British law gives tenants inordinate rights if there is a dispute, and so we had to relocate our program; we rented space in Oxford. The students were primarily from the Middle East - India, Saudi Arabia, Pakistan - they were not English students. Many of them had purchased homes in Bushy and didn't want to drive fifty miles to Oxford. As a result, enrollment started going down, and we closed it in the Spring 1993 and arranged a teach out.

When I first came, Rust called one night and asked if I could come to his house the next day. At that point, this being about the third or fourth week I was here, I thought if I could negotiate with this guy and reach some kind of an amicable settlement about the controversy over the London campus, I'd do it. So, I went to his house one Saturday; when I got there, he had documents all over the furniture in the living room, most of them WASC related. He was trying to convince me that he was the innocent party and that this big bad WASC had it in for him. He invited me out there one other time to try to convince me that all the financial problems had not been his fault. Shortly after that we started negotiating, and the relationship fell apart pretty quickly.

I was speaking once at the Kiwanis Club downtown - that is one of the things I did early on, to get myself into every possible city group I could - and in the Q and A period, one of the members said, 'Is Bill Rust still at the University?' I responded with a no, and three people in the room simultaneously said, 'Good!' I still hear the Bill Rust stories but not as much because I had what I called my 'clearing of the deck speech.' Now when I am out, I don't hear any more Bill Rust stories. When I came, I used to get a question about why I took the job; now the comments are that they are hearing about the interesting things that are going on at the University.

[What were the major steps in turning around the $28 million debt?] We had to be creative to do that, because we had only a year to do it. The reorganization plan was put in place in 1990 by Ken and a new Board - the Board was here, and we have added to the Board since I came. There are only two people on the Board from the Rust era, and one was the Chair when I came - he had been a relatively new member in the late 80s and was one of the two Board members who, in 1989, went to Rust and said it was time to leave. When Rust left, it was a small Board that met only once or twice a year, and they were cronies, by and large. So when he left, most of the old Board disappeared. The remaining Board members and McLennan, as the Acting President, recruited some new members. They decided that the best way to give the University some time to survive was to seek protection under Chapter 11. They did that in 1990. The plan that was confirmed by the Court was a three-year plan that said the University had to be out of debt by November 1993 or auction off the campus to get whatever money it could to pay off creditors.

I don't think an auction would have been very successful - this is very limited use property, and the residents in the community are adamantly opposed to any development that would put more people on Pomerado Road or more kids in the schools. So while this is choice space in one way - for an office park or the like - it is otherwise very limited choice space. It is zoned residential but with a conditional use permit for education, and to get that changed to sell it to a commercial enterprise or auction it off seemed remote. But, even if successful, I took the position that an auction to pay off the secured creditors here would be the same as closing the institution. All this place needed then was one more headline saying USIU was auctioning its property after all the headlines saying USIU may close, USIU declares bankruptcy. The public was not going to separate an auction from a closing.

So, for six months, I listened to a number of wild and exotic schemes from people who thought they had ideas about what to do with the property. A lot of stuff came out of the woodwork. There were even some foreign investors who had purchased other campuses - Teikyo, I think was the name. Before I came, they had some contact with McLennan and expressed some interest in buying the campus. I don't know what really happened to that, but by the time I came, they had gone away. Then there was a group from Taiwan that approached me about buying the campus, but in my judgment that was not realistic and wouldn't work. Also I didn't think we could get WASC approval for a change of control. I think one of the things Ken told me about Teikyo is that WASC was concerned that it would be controlled not by people primarily involved in education.

After six months, we realized we had about six months to go and that we had better get moving to solve this problem. And, there weren't any good prospects. Therefore I approached the Chairman of the group of private, non-profit companies within which I had worked for ten years before coming to USIU. To make a long story short, another non-profit company was formed within that group for the purpose of purchasing the USIU campus. Then, to make it more than just a landlord-tenant relationship, we developed an affiliation with that organization, which under California non-profit corporate law, became the Member of the USIU corporation, which is non-profit, and we remain non-profit.

If we were for profit, you could use the analogy of a holding company and its subsidiary. But, under California non-profit law, there are certain things a Member could do in that relationship if we were outside of education, so when we wrote the agreement, the Member gave up some of its legal rights. For example, the Member in a non-profit world can appoint the CEO of an affiliate organization, can change Bylaws at will, and appoint directors to the Board. What we did when we wrote the agreement was to say that the Board of USIU continues to appoint the CEO, so if I were to leave, it would be the Board of USIU that would appoint my successor. With respect to the Bylaws, the University agreed that the Member could change them unless two-thirds of the members of the USIU Board objected to the change. As to the appointment of members to the Board of Trustees, the USIU Board nominates trustees to the Member, and the Member selects from among the nominees.

Also to make it a long term relationship, the USIU corporation leases the campus back under a master lease from the Member. This yielded enough money to pay off the secured creditors. The arrangement is such that USIU pays rent to the Member (our affiliate partner) in an amount equal to six percent of our tuition income on an annual basis. To satisfy the Court and the unsecured creditors, we said that for seven years (this started in November, 1993 and will end in February, 2001), instead of all that six percent going to HRS, Inc., only three percent would, the other three percent will go into a fund to be used to be spread over the unsecured creditors. The unsecured creditors could see they were going to get something, even if not one hundred cents on the dollar. They weren't particularly happy, but the Court said, realistically, if the secureds get paid and the unsecureds get something, that's enough. The Court accepted that deal and that ended the bankruptcy.

[*Did your work with the community take time ?*] I'd say it is still going on although it has become less a change in image than in gaining visibility. The image change is certainly different and is not a problem today. The ongoing issue is visibility. If you are going to have a problem with one or the other, I'd much rather have it one of lack of visibility than poor image - at least you are starting with a clean slate.

You know, we sit here in a city dominated by UC [University of California]-San Diego [UCSD] and San Diego State University [SDSU], and to some extent by the University of San Diego [USD]. To the extent there is visibility in the news, it is always SDSU first and UCSD second, and, ironically, USD has some of the same problems we do. San Diego State gets the play - they have the athletic teams.

We had the head education reporter of the influential *The Union Tribune* on campus, and we talked about that. He is not hostile to this place - when I came, he did a very nice feature on me, and when we got out of debt and got Chapter 11 behind us, he did a very nice feature on the University. But, our PR person can pitch something to him, and nothing will happen to it, but then we will read about something very similar that happened at San Diego State. For example, one of our faculty got a $100,000 grant, but that wasn't newsworthy. Two weeks later, somebody at San Diego State got a $50,000 grant, and that was newsworthy. The reporter was very candid about it and said that San Diego State was the biggest institution in town and has a lot of alumni who stay in San Diego. So, it becomes a numbers game, and we work on that.

But, the image turnaround took longer for two reasons - the bad image was so deep and so broad. Everybody had heard about or read about troubles at USIU. And when the good news started happening, it was not necessarily newsworthy. The only thing that was newsworthy was when we got out of Chapter 11, but the other things didn't make it.

It is an ongoing process. I still spend a lot of time in the broader community. But, it is changing. We had a PR firm do a little survey of the movers and shakers in San Diego, people who have some area of influence, including those with whom I have had an opportunity to talk and those with whom I haven't. We found, fortunately, what we expected to find: if we had had an opportunity to be with people, talk to them, and tell them what is going on, the feedback about their impressions of USIU was quite different from those with whom we have not yet been in contact. But, it told us our strategy was working - getting to people, telling them what is going on. But, it also tells us that we're not there yet, we're not home scot free. There are still a lot of people out there who don't know who we are and those who still think we are what we were. It will take a long time for the good to overcome the bad. It's terribly ingrained.

On the favorable side, there are a lot of new people in San Diego in the bioscience and high-tech areas. San Diego is becoming to bioscience what Silicon Valley was to computers. As these people come, they do so with none of the negative history. As these people come in, they come in fresh - they have none of the history, so as we meet them and tell them who we are, it' s a matter of them becoming acquainted with us as opposed to having to overcome the negative image.

The media know me in other ways, but not well. There are two influential business papers here, *The Union Tribune* is the one I was referring to earlier in my discussion with the reporter about coverage, and *The San Diego Business Journal*, which is a weekly, highly respected business journal. The *Journal* does a business profile every week and did a profile of me about two years ago. That got a lot of mileage. From time to time, they cover us, especially about our international business program. There is also the *Daily Transcript*, which did a profile on me, a turn around story that really helped. *San Diego Magazine* featured me along with 30 other CEOs in town not too long ago. So that kind of visibility is helping. However, *The Union Tribune* is the old thing - if you can't make the sports page, you can't make it any · place else.

As I already mentioned, McLennan got rid of the overloaded sports program, which permitted me to get back on a modest basis. A few years ago, I started men's and women's tennis, then men's and women's soccer; last year it was men's and women's cross-country, and in the current year women's volleyball. As we have done this, we've gotten coverage on the sports pages. We hired a top flight, women's tennis pro, who had retired from the circuit, as tennis coach. Since she was known by the sports writers, when we hired her, they did a big feature on her. When we started volleyball, we hired an ex-player, an alumna from here some years ago and who was recognized as a top-flight volleyball player - that got good press also.

The first building I would have built would not have been a sports center. But, we got a freebie. We provided the land, and somebody else built the building. We have exclusive use of one basketball court, which is convertible into two volleyball courts, and also full access when the building is not in use. Our tenant group is called High Five-America; among other things, they run basketball camps for high school kids in the summer. So it was a win-win situation. We get a free recreational facility and three hundred high school kids coming on campus each week when they are in their program. So we get visibility. We also rent the facility - there is a kind of second-line, minor pro-basketball team that has started here in town. They don't play their games here but use the facility for practice. So the sports writers come out and cover them.

The construction of the center is quite different - it's a fabric top. When the construction workers installed it, they just got up there and rolled out twenty foot wide sheets and then zipped it up at the top. That was different enough so we had the press out to watch the process. But, it's the same old thing - for sports we get coverage, for a grant or something academic, we don't.

[*How did you get your corporate experience and how did it impact your role as CEO of USIU?*] Dick Hawk, who is the president of HRS, Inc with which we are affiliated, was the first Executive Director of the Higher Education Coordinating Board of Minnesota, the old 1202 Commission. He had been assistant dean in the graduate College of Education at the University of Chicago and was hired by the Board in the mid-60s. He predated me since I didn't go to Minnesota until 1971. Our offices were right across the hall in the same building, so with his heading the State coordinating board and I involved with the state university system, we had a lot of contact with program approvals, budget issues, and state-wide policies. Then he left in 1976 to found the first of what became several corporations, all of which had something to do with student loan business.

Dick called me one day and said he wanted to share the executive responsibilities and would I be interested in coming. So, I got intrigued about being involved again in building something new and having a new experience. So, I went with him and thought I would be with him until I retired. But, then the student loan business started changing. One of our businesses was as a guarantee agency. A lot of the large lenders like Bank of America and City Bank started bringing us a lot of paper junk from for-profit proprietary schools with huge default rates. The federal government took the position that if you are going to guarantee loans for four-year institutions you would have to guarantee loans for any student a lender brings. It got to the point that it became ludicrous. We had the largest student loan portfolio in the country of any guarantee agency, because we were not just a state agency as in California, but were a private, non-profit. Our default rate on the proprietary schools was 41 percent! If you're an insurance company, and you have a bad risk, you could increase your rates. However, the government limited the maximum we could charge to 2 percent. As that started to change, Hawk began to think it wasn't worth it. So instead of building, we started to level out.

Frankly, I think that corporate experience was one of the factors that was appealing to the Board. They liked that combination, and to me, personally, it has been invaluable. We recognize that this is an educational institution and therefore it can't be run exactly like a corporation, but we also recognize that we are bottom-line oriented. If we don't have strong management, we're not going to make it, especially in a place like this, to survive as an educational institution. So I think those ten years in business have helped me personally and professionally.

The other way it has helped is in the business community. As they have gotten to know me and become aware of my background, I'm not viewed just as an academic type. I've gotten fairly significantly involved with the Chamber of Commerce and sit on its Public Policy Committee, the Board of Directors, and chair its International Business Forum. Many of them know that I have been in business, so they can look at me as one of them.

Would You Do It Again?

Yeah, I would. This is the eighth year and it doesn't seem like it, frankly. Obviously, as you know, there are times when it can get frustrating, and you say are we ever going to get this done or that done. But, yeah, I'd do it in a minute. It has been an extremely rewarding experience. I thought if we could pull it off in a situation like this, to really have an impact and to see the results would be great - and it has been.

When I left the state university system in Minnesota, I thought I would probably never go back into education; it wasn't that I left disenchanted with higher education. In fact, I wasn't even looking to leave. But, I had been doing that for eleven years.

I think many of us don't really plan our careers. In my case, as I look back on it, I tended to be open to other possibilities especially as the job became routine and administrative as opposed to growing or building or changing and having an opportunity to make an impact. So again, while I wasn't looking to come back into higher education, the job I was doing was more routine and administrative rather than management and development. So when Ginny [Lester]called me, I was more open to a situation where there was clearly a lot to do.

Dr. Alan E. Guskin, Antioch University

The Institution

Antioch University, founded in 1852 and located in Yellow Springs, Ohio, is an independent, non-profit institution It is classified as a Baccalaureate - Liberal Arts institution, but this designation applies only to Antioch College. Four other units of the University offer graduate programs, including the doctorate in one; hence the correct Carnegie Classification should be Doctoral Research Intensive. At the time of the interview, the combined on- and off-campus enrollment was about 3,000, with about 500 students in Antioch College, which, as noted above, is to close in 2008.

Founded as a private, co-educational liberal arts institution, the College's first president was Horace Mann (1853-1859), long recognized as the father of the American public school system. The College has endeavored to inculcate in its students Mann's challenge to the graduating class of 1859, "Be ashamed to die until you have won some victory for humanity." Throughout its history, Antioch distinguished itself as one of the country's leading innovators in higher education. It was among the first colleges to admit women as equal to men (Oberlin College was the first in 1830), and one of the first to admit African-Americans. The introduction of work-study programs in 1921 broke tradition, making Antioch unique among liberal arts colleges of the day.

Antioch University is now comprised of Antioch College and McGregor School (established 1988) in Yellow Springs, Antioch New England Graduate School in Keene, New Hampshire (1964), Antioch University Seattle, Washington (1975), and Antioch University Southern California in Los Angeles (1972) and Santa Barbara (1977). During the period from 1964 to 1975, the College expanded to some thirty-four centers; from 1976 to 1985, the number of centers was reduced to eight (plus the College), and between 1986 and 1997 those were further reduced to the present configuration.

The core of Antioch's educational mission is a focus on the individual learner and on the belief that the role of education is to help students in the purposeful pursuit of a meaningful life. To that end, Antioch's legacy is tied to its values - values that allow students to validate their life experiences, challenge their beliefs, and ultimately act on those values to help improve society.

Students in Antioch College are required to alternate classroom study with five work/cooperative experiences, one of which must be cross-cultural. The other components of the University offer combinations of undergraduate, graduate, and teacher certification programs for adult learners.

Upon appointment in 1985, Alan Guskin became the seventeenth president. The longest in tenure, Arthur Morgan, served fifteen years (the last two concurrently as head of the Tennessee Valley Authority). His immediate predecessor, William Birenbaum, served for nine years. Guskin served as President of the University from 1985-94 and concurrently as President of Antioch College. Following a major restructuring, he served as Chancellor of the five campus University from 1994-97. In 1997, he became a Distinguished University Professor as well as being named President Emeritus of Antioch University.

Alan E. Guskin

Alan Guskin received a BA in Psychology (Honors) from Brooklyn College in 1958 and a PhD in Social Psychology from the University of Michigan in 1968.

His varied teaching experience included: Instructor in Psychology and Research, Chulalongkorn University, Bangkok, when he served as a Peace Corps Volunteer (1962-64); Lecturer, Department of Psychology (1968-71) and Associate Professor, Department of Behavioral Sciences (1971), University of Michigan; Associate Professor (1971-73) and Professor (1973-75), Departments of Sociology and Education, Clark University; Professor of Education, University of Wisconsin-Parkside (1975-85); University Professor, Antioch University (1985-97); and Chair,

Higher Education Institutes, Teachers College, Columbia University (1997-99). He also served as a member of the faculty of the Institute for Educational Management, Harvard University (Summers 1986, 1987, 1988).

Guskin's administrative experience is also varied and included: Selection Officer, Peace Corps (Summer 1961); Director, Division of Selection, VISTA (1964-65); Director, Florida Migrant Farm Worker Program, St. Petersburg, FL (1965-66); Project Director and Acting Assistant Director, Center for Research on Utilization of Scientific Knowledge, Institute for Social Research, University of Michigan (1968-70); Project Director, Education Change Team, College of Education, University of Michigan (1970-71); Provost (1971-73) and Acting President (1973-74), Clark University; and Chancellor, University of Wisconsin-Parkside (1975-85).

In addition to six books (*e.g.*, A Social Psychology of Education; New Directions for Teaching and Learning: The Administrator's Role in Effective Teaching), he is the author of more than 25 articles in a range of journals (*e.g., Change, Trusteeship, Liberal Learning, American Journal of Orthopsychiatry*) and gave keynote and major addresses at various regional and national meetings (*e.g.,* American Association for Higher Education Summer Academy, National Academy for Academic Leadership, American Association of University Administrators). He served as a consultant to a number of institutions including Portland State University, University of Wisconsin-Milwaukee, Olivet College, California State University-Monterey Bay, among many others. He also served on the boards and/or committees of the American Association of State Colleges and Universities, American Council on Education, Great Lakes Colleges Association, University of North Carolina-Asheville, and Pierson-Lovelace Foundation, among many others.

Guskin received an Honorary Doctor of Laws from Saybrook Institute (1989) and an Honorary Doctor of Humane Letters from Antioch University (1997).

Alan Guskin's comments that follow are a transcript of his interview on January 14, 2000 in his office on the Antioch University Seattle campus. The questions that prompted his comments have either been omitted or are indicated within parentheses

The Situation and the Turnaround

I made the decision to come to Antioch in March 1985, left the University of Wisconsin-Parkside on August 1st, and became President on September 1. It was extraordinary. For years, people would ask, 'Why did you take the job?' My wife at the time was opposed to it, my friends were opposed to it, Allan Ostar opposed it. [Ostar was then President of the American Association of State Colleges and Universities (AASCU).] At the time, I was on the AASCU Board and may have become the next Chair. So, a lot of people opposed the move.

The place was a disaster, an unmitigated disaster. Even today, there is no rational reason why I took the job. The only thing one can say is that it was an incredible challenge. Historically, it had been a great institution, but it had been so badly managed for so many years that it was almost destroyed, and mostly because of inadequate systems. People didn't seem to know what they were doing. But, it was a difficult institution to run. Here I was leaving Parkside with a palatial office, a gorgeous facility, a lovely place; I was forty-eight and had been there ten years.

It was an extraordinary thing. In the middle of the campus were two of the six major buildings in a horseshoe arrangement that were closed. There were other closed buildings. Across the street, or green, that the main building looked out on, was the campus recycling center with garbage flowing over its barrels. It was absolutely incredible. The residence halls were an unmitigated disaster, all but one. So it was quite extraordinary. And the College had only four hundred students. With the co-op program, a 30 to 40 percent of the students were away, there were no more than two hundred and twenty. This was a campus that once had twelve hundred students. It was quite something.

I had been a Peace Corps Volunteer in the early 60s; a friend, Joe Kauffman, told me I was still a Peace Corps Volunteer. But, it was a great mission. And, there were a lot of issues I was not aware of until after I came. But most fascinating, two weeks in, I really wondered why I did it. I didn't tell that to a soul for a year, not until much later on.

I walked the campus for several days; I am not a person to be frightened, but I was a little scared and wondered if I had made a career error. Here I had brought my family into this in a little town in Ohio. Then on the second or third day, I came back into my office and talked with the vice president who had been at Antioch quite a number of years, and I said, 'Jack, we are not going down with a whimper; if we go down it will be in flames.'

Then I made a couple of momentous decisions to take control of the institution. That was the big issue, nobody was in control. It became clear very quickly, and I think if I hadn't had ten years as a president before, it would have been hard to figure out as fast that it wasn't the financial problem that was driving the institution even though the place was essentially bankrupt and twelve months away from closing. You can't believe the things they did - trying not to pay bills, not paying taxes, borrowing everything right to the hilt, borrowing money from trustees - all the crazy things, terrible, terrible stuff. I looked at the books and couldn't figure out why there was such a terrible problem until I realized they weren't collecting tuition dollars beyond say 85 to 90 percent. So, on a $20 million budget, they were down $2 million just for starts. We were $2 million in the red, the students weren't paying although the books said so. And the administration wasn't hanging tough about collecting at registration. I said that is an easy thing to solve.

The other thing, people were overrunning their budgets. I said that is an easy thing to solve also. In the public sector, as in Wisconsin, you don't overrun your budget, that would be the equivalent of a misappropriation of state dollars. You live within your means. The chief financial officer of the University asked my attitude about balanced budgets. I said I don't have an attitude; it's something you do, it is not an option - you just do it, there is no choice.

It was extraordinary. This was in September, and the first Board meeting was on October 15, six weeks later. When I came into that Board meeting, I did two things that blew people's minds. One, I said we are closing the Law School. It had been established in 1972 and, of all the units, was seen as the most powerful and politically, a very, very difficult place. While other law schools were making money hand over fist, this one was losing money by not collecting tuition and all kinds of crazy stuff. My predecessor had fought for a number of years in the courts to try to wrest control of the Law School from the Deans, spending hundreds of thousands of dollars at a time when the place was bankrupt. When I came in, I realized that the ABA [American Bar Association] was going to withdraw accreditation, and before I became president, I went to an ABA meeting and said you can't take such action until I as the new president make a decision about its future. They realized then that we could not afford to lose accreditation of the Law School. It was an unviable place - quality of the faculty, quality of the students. I said to myself, this will keep for a month or two, but I needed to take control of the institution, which was spinning out of control.

I said the College is critical. We have to rebuild the College, that is not an option - there is no Antioch without the College. I said we can't rebuild the College and the Law School at the same time. So, I decided to close the Law School at the first Board meeting.

Then what happened was interesting. Closing the Law School made some of the Trustees extraordinarily upset. So, I told the Chair, who was totally in favor of it but didn't have the guts to do it, that I was not going to politic for this decision, that it was his responsibility. I told him that tonight when I will be having the dinner party at my house, I would not politic, but that he should. I said, "That's why I announced it before the dinner." He came to me at the end of the evening saying it was twelve to six in my favor.

The next morning there was an emergency meeting of the Executive Committee called by the Vice Chair, who was opposed to the decision. He pointed a finger at me and said I couldn't do this, and I said I can count, I have the votes. So we were fighting back and forth while the rest of the Board was waiting. One of the other members asked, 'What do we have to do to convince you not to do this?' I said, 'You give me a unanimous vote to do whatever I need to do and whenever I want to do it.' They gave me such a vote, and I closed the Law School six months later. Then everybody knew someone was in control.

The other thing I did was to get the Board to pass a resolution that we will have a balanced budget no matter what the pain. The next day I went to the Vice President for Finance and said, 'Tell me how we do this.' He said we can't do this, and I reminded him that the Board had passed a balanced budget resolution no matter what the pain. I said this should be a godsend to you as a finance officer. He said we couldn't do it. So, I said, 'OK, at five o'clock today, all expenditures by the University are suspended, and any expenditure must bear my personal signature.' He said, 'You can't be serious.' I said I was serious and was going to do it. They started doing all kinds of crazy things to test it, sending me expenditures for $2.35, but they knew I was serious. They would say, 'Are you going to sign this?', and I said, 'Yes, watch me.' And, I signed it very slowly.

The year before I came, there was an $800,000 deficit; the next year there was a $600,000 surplus. It wasn't a financial problem, it was a human problem. Understanding that, for me, changed everything. The Dean in San Francisco overran his budget, so we fired him. He asked why I was asking for his resignation and began to give reasons for being out of budget. I told him, 'I understood that but I don't have the money. We had a policy, you overran your budget, and you have to leave. There is no good reason because, as you know, I don't print money, and who is going to pay those bills?' There was never a budget overrun from June 1986 until a new president of the College came in September 1994. No one would dare overrun a budget - it was as if there was this myth about what would happen if they did, that they would implode if they did. This powerful discipline allowed us to start rebuilding the institution.

Beyond closing the Law School, we had to close two campuses that were marginal quality-wise and financially; that was in June 1988. From 1985-1988, the only big increases in budgets were at the College, which experienced a 25 percent increase in enrollment. In 1988, we also began funding the College up front rather than have it in deficit, but we disciplined the College to stay within its means as well. We spent perhaps $1 to $1.5 million each year on the College, with the rest of the University supporting it. But that was legitimate.

Those were the kinds of huge decisions we made in the first few years to get the University under control, redirect it, and focus on rebuilding the College. Everybody knew what the mantra was - building quality in the adult campuses, building a good faculty with fair faculty salaries. Everybody knew what the strategy was and that we were serious about it.

In June 1988, we closed the Philadelphia and San Francisco campuses and completed the final closing of the Law School. We built one new campus in Yellow Springs for adult learners. We combined the Los Angeles and Santa Barbara units into one administrative unit that is called Southern California. That makes five campuses, each headed by a president but, at the time I came, they were headed by a dean, then provosts, and, by the time I left, the Board was considering the change to president. The College head was a president in 1994, the others became presidents in 1998. The chief executive of the University is called Chancellor. The University structure is very decentralized, much more so than ever before.

[*Account for the growth of Antioch College from 400 students*] I think the key issue to the lack of growth of Antioch College was that a lot of people were not doing their jobs - in admissions, for example. The tragic thing, one of the saddest of all, is that a lot of the pain of prior years was unnecessary. It wasn't that people were ill-intentioned, it's that they just didn't know what they were supposed to do. It is incredible to describe their behavior - some were lacking in experience, some being too ideological and basically not knowing what they had to do. It was devastating.

The College enrollment went from four hundred to six hundred because we answered the mail, the admissions people formed associations, we did some of the things admissions offices do. When we were down below 600, you could watch the burnout of the admissions people. When we brought in new people, it took about a year to eighteen months, and the enrollment began to go up. It's now in the mid 700s, which is not a bad number. As long as the enrollment hovers between 700 and 800, it can pretty much operate as long as it has the University to back it up.

A lot of institutions float in and out over a five to seven year period. Antioch went into the doldrums in 1972-73, and I came in 1985. Antioch is particularly vulnerable because of what I call powerful centrifugal forces. The students are mavericks, it's a politically left institution, and the eighteen and nineteen year olds imagine what is happening, that authorities are against them, and they are fighting their fathers and uncles and who knows what. So, it was very difficult to lead the place. And, sometimes the faculty joined the students so you have a very complex institution even though it is very small. If you expand that to other campuses, you have the same thing. If you go out in the halls here in Seattle and ask faculty what the values of Antioch are, people who have been here eighteen months talk as if they have been at Antioch fourteen or fifteen years.

[*Comment about the Board and micromanagement*] When I arrived, the Board was exhausted, and there was a lot of micromanagement. The Board was composed of a lot of the College's graduates, almost 100 percent the year before I was chosen, and that is why they got rid of my predecessor - because they felt he didn't like the College and that the College (and University) was being badly hurt. They finally overwhelmed him. The Board members wanted to do good, but one of the problems I've learned about Boards is that while people who serve on boards are very often business people, when they come to a university, they seem to leave their management skills at the door and too often they do things they know are wrong. But their hearts were leading them. These Board members just loved the College. If there was a problem, they'd say, 'We'll solve it.' without realizing they should not be doing the president's work. I had to explain to the Board that I would not permit any micromanaging and that I was to be held accountable. If you are developing the budget, and I present it to the Board, you can't hold me accountable because you have already been co-opted.

That is what was happening. They were into it. They were going around the country with the chief financial officer of the University developing the budget with the various campuses. There was no accountability. As I noted earlier, if we collect tuition at only 90 percent, we should spend at 90 percent - you can't spend 100 percent, it won't work. The Board Chair was telling me to run a deficit of 10 percent, and I said of course we can do it but shouldn't. Further the chair of the finance committee was one of the people going around the country to the different campuses and helping to develop campus budgets.

The Board had gotten into a bad state of mind, which was the result of poor University leadership. They had become confused about what their role was as a lay board. They had to be educated. So I told them about Kingman Brewster's three G's - Give, Get or Go. I said, 'Give money, get money, or leave the Board, but you don't manage. You hired me to run the institution, and you have to hold me accountable to do so.' One of the members said, 'But I wasn't put on the Board to go out and get money; I came on to help manage the institution.'

It was very sad - the Board got confused. Good people, loaning money to the institution, taking second mortgages on their houses without telling their spouses. It was unbelievable - and there was no directors' insurance. These Board members were so vulnerable, it was absolutely incredible. And, because of that, you couldn't get certain people to come on the Board. They became exhausted. These people were CEOs of companies working at hard jobs who came here three times a year for Board meetings and then were asked to travel around the country, working on budgets, being asked to loan money. They were physically and psychologically exhausted.

I think I played some role changing the mode of operation and strengthening and diversifying the Board, but the real credit goes to the Chair of the Board that I helped select. Being involved in his selection was probably something I shouldn't have done, but he did a marvelous job. We worked in tandem - we talked about it -

he shared my values about what a Board should be. When he became chair, that was in my third year, he took responsibility for the Board. That was a mistake in some ways because it caused tension later when I didn't spend much time with the Board. I had good relations with the Board but didn't communicate a lot with them as individuals. The Chair was the communication link, and at times he was in competition with me. We worked it out. He was Chair of the Board for six years, and on balance, he was absolutely marvelous. He allowed me the time to spend working inside the institution as well as raising money, and he took care of management of the Board.

I had a lot to do in the background regarding who became members of the Board, and I had a lot to do with my presentation of what my role was and what the Board's role was. For example, once a Board member told me that I was an executive director, and therefore the Board should tell me what to do. I responded, 'You didn't hire an executive director, you hired a President - if you want an executive director, you have to look for somebody else.' That never came up again.

Early on, I had to do that kind of stuff, which, five or six years later, cost me because a few of the Board members never forgave me. By the end of my stay there were four or five board members who were really difficult. Out of twenty-five members, that may not seem much, but as you know, four or five can make a difference in the climate of a Board meeting. I always had the votes, and they didn't, so I never had to worry seriously about anything. But it was niggling stuff here and there, and every now and then, things would begin to spin out of control, and the Board Chair would have to move in. Nothing comes free, and that was the price of being quite directive and very clear very early on. I know I made a few mistakes at various points that didn't help my relationship with some of the Board members.

If it is ok, I would like to make some general observations. For example, I came away from Antioch feeling that small institutions are extraordinarily vulnerable. Big universities essentially run by themselves; as the President of the University of Michigan, what can you do? For small institutions, you just watch them jump up and down depending on the quality of their leadership.

There is something about Antioch that attracts certain kinds of people. It tends to be those who want to create anew and are not very respectful of what came before, which is very positive sometimes, but they are very wedded to the institution's values. There is a lot of tension, so leading such an institution is very complicated. You have to remember that the centrifugal forces are OK, but they have to be balanced by centripetal forces. You have to create boundaries, because you know young students constantly push against boundaries, and if there are no boundaries they keep on pushing until they find one. Some leaders didn't understand that, and so they joined the students in the 70s, and it blew the place apart. It is very sad that the President joined the students in believing that they could remake the institution.

I believe that the presidency is inherently a conservative position, being the steward of the history and values of the institution. If you don't like that, leave. That's your job. For me it's a wonderful, noble mission. So the tragedy of Antioch is that a good many of the crises and the devastating conditions were not necessary.

The answer for a lot of these issues is for people to understand that it is OK to have left-oriented values, and it is OK to challenge authority, but you have to manage the institution. That's what I think I brought because I have a peculiar set of attitudes and skills. I'm a maverick and always have been, but I always lived within the borders of institutions. Even in the heyday of the 1960s, I was a close friend of Tom Hayden and some of the people in SDS [Students for a Democratic Society], but I was never a radical. I was always a liberal friend, which was not a compliment in those days. I always believed my role was internal to the institution, and that was my skill. I was always responsive to those external groups and could respond to them because I shared a lot of common values, but I was always very much of the institution and shared those values. I was a maverick, sometimes questioning authority and never felt bad when people questioned authority because I knew if I were they, I would be doing the same thing. So I smiled about it and related to them.

But I combined that with sometimes being a SOB as an administrator.

In an article I wrote for *Psychologist-Manager* about my role as a chief executive, I discussed how it is possible to be a strong leader in an inherently collaborative institution - in the sense I have been describing about the decisions I was making and people letting me do it. In my first two years, I would meet with the College's governance committee, which was composed of students, faculty, and administrators, and I would lay out the budget and say, 'This is what it should be.' I did not have the time nor energy to deal with a highly collaborative budget process - but they would never let me get away with that four or five years later, nor would I try.

The question is how can an institution that was (and is) so egalitarian permit someone to do that - I was a tough, high profile leader those first three or so years. My answer is that everybody knew that if the systems weren't built, controls weren't in place, and that there wasn't somebody giving them some hope and a sense of direction, the place was not going to make it. So they gave me that freedom, but once things were getting healthy, we went back to a more collaborative, collegial decision-making style, which is more my natural style anyway. People wondered whether I could give up the strong, directive leadership style, but that was easy because I didn't like some of the implications of some of the things that I had to do. My leadership style evolved at Antioch, but it was amazing that an egalitarian institution like Antioch allowed itself to be led so strongly because people knew it had to be done if we were to be successful.

[*In the survey, you said, "You have to have the passion and commitment to the values of an institution."*] Absolutely. I think back to the three institutions of which I was president [University of Wisconsin-Parkside and then Antioch] or acting president [Clark University]. At Clark, a lot of people pushed me to become President, and I thought at that point, when I was thirty-six or thirty-seven, that I wanted it. But it would have been a mistake because I didn't share the institution's values, which were really quite conservative. And, some senior faculty knew that better than I knew it. There was a lot of tension between the selection committee, the Board Chair, and some very powerful senior faculty over whether I would be named president. So I withdrew my candidacy because eventually I knew I wasn't going to get it. I didn't understand or know it until later that the faculty were absolutely right. I shouldn't have been President at Clark - at my core, I really didn't share the values of the institution so it would have been more a case of my acting as President rather than being President.

At Parkside, it was fascinating because I had to hide some of my values from the community. They liked me a lot, I was very outgoing, and the institution was young - only seven years old. But when I got there, the University was moribund and didn't have a good relationship with the community. I had some big challenges there early on. Some of the business leaders saw me as a New York Jew with a beard and assumed I was a Communist. I tried to disabuse them of that. Afterwards, they saw me differently after a lecture on academic freedom and a few other things, they saw me very differently. They respected that I was tough and that they weren't going to push me around. So here I was with this young, vibrant institution, but the money and power in the community was not progressive at all. I did well, I learned my trade. I made close links with all parts of the community. We made major strides in the quality of the faculty and academic programs. I loved it, it was a kick, it was a fun thing to do, and I was protected by the University of Wisconsin System.

Being on my own, as I was at Antioch, the message at Clark came back. I really embodied and understood at a core level the alignment of values at Antioch. When I went out to talk about Antioch, there was a lot of authenticity. People saw me talking about issues and responding to their questions, looking me in the eye to check out whether I was really a true Antiochian. They liked what they saw because I really shared the values of the institution. I think if you really don't share the values of an institution it is much harder to be a real steward. And that is so much of what we do as presidents.

The finance, administrative functions, and fundraising stuff are all part of the job, a big part of the job, but the real issue is your symbolic role, what I call 'the priestly function.' Ultimately the symbolic role makes you effective and extraordinarily powerful. It's a sheer joy, and you never use it up. No one ever gets angry with you for representing the institution. So embodying the values enables you to steward in a very powerful way. I have come to believe that it is a key part of being a president, especially of a value-driven institution. There are institutions in which it doesn't make a difference but at Antioch it did. Any place that really holds its values up front, you really have to buy in big time.

[*In the survey, you indicated that one must have experience and leadership skills but also courage and guts.*] Bob Krinsky, who became Board Chair, and I became very close friends, said to me, 'Are you ready to do this? What happens if we vote against you?' He was standing no farther away from me than you are, and I said, 'You would have to look for a new president.' At the time it seemed more courageous to observers than it did to me. Because I did what I normally would do. If they didn't want me to do this and voted to overrule me on the first series of core decisions, this would not be the place for me to be. If this were my first job maybe I would have been different. But, I am not a cautious person, and after ten years as Chancellor at Parkside, I knew what I had to do at Antioch. But also I had no fear about getting another job. I had a good track record.

Being a president does take a lot of guts and courage as well as a lot of compassion. But, if you have guts and no compassion, I think you will have a negative impact on the institution. Usually, such a person tends to be dismissive and even abusive of those who disagree. Being a president is a very humbling role and represents for me the highest leadership role one can perform. You are dealing with the minds of people and creating an institution in which people can grow and create. It is just an incredible responsibility and honor to serve. And sometimes I jokingly say, but I am really quite serious, that for the privilege of leading others, the gods exact a price.

Rebuilding institutions is not getting any easier, the pains and struggles are becoming more commonplace, I would like to find out how to help presidential colleagues, to coach them, not just from my own experience but from theirs as well. One of the things about being a president of a small institution is that you are involved in lots of kinds of activities and functions - not like the president of a very large institution - and you have experience in all these different kinds of things. The presidents of small institutions know so much about so many kinds of things. I believe it is tragic that there isn't within the educational system mechanisms for sharing among leaders. In the business world, there are coaches galore, every chief executive seems to have a coach. In higher education we don't have such a thing. Everybody assumes they can do the job even if they have never done it before and know nothing about the institution. It's absurd. Everybody thinks that when you start a new presidency you are going to be effective even if you have little experience in carrying out the duties of the office.

Would You Do It Again?

Yes, I would. It sounds crazy but I cannot imagine being a leader of any other institution than Antioch at that point of time that would have given me more meaning. In terms of a sense of purpose, there is nothing that will ever match that. If you create a new institution, maybe you can have the kind of experience I had, but, true or not, I feel I was literally President at a critical moment in the life of a great institution and what I did really made a difference. That doesn't mean nobody else could have done it. But I was the one who did it, and so that gives me an enormous, extraordinary sense of meaning in life. It is something that gives me a sense of peace. It is very special. And, yes, I would do it again. But would I want to go through, if I had a choice, all the pain I went through? No, I'd prefer not to. But the truth is you can't have meaning without the pain. The level of feeling that you have accomplished so much in the critical moments in the life of an institution does not come without a price. The gods do exact a price for giving you the privilege of leading others.

During the last few years, I still loved the work but it was getting monotonous. But, before that, I used to tell myself that what I was doing was not just for the people here today but for the future, the president's role is for the future. I loved it, it was a kick.

Dr. Stephen C. Morgan, University of La Verne

The University

The University of La Verne, founded in 1891 and located in La Verne, California, is an independent, non-profit, Doctoral Research/Intensive institution. The University has off-campus sites in seven locations in California (including three on military bases), two in Alaska, and one each in Greece, Singapore, and Taiwan. The combined on-and off-campus enrollment is about 8,000, with some 1,100 students on the main campus.

The University was founded as Lordsburg College by members of the Church of the Brethren who had moved from the Midwest to settle a new land. Both the College and the agricultural community were renamed La Verne in 1917. During the subsequent three decades, three quarters of the students were in teacher education. In 1933, the College became independent of church control. It awarded its first masters degree in 1965 and first doctorate in 1979. In 1969, the College began offering degree programs off campus and opened its College of Law in 1970. It reorganized as the University of La Verne in 1977. In the following years, the San Fernando College of Law became part of the University, and the San Fernando Valley Center was established (1983). The San Fernando College of Law was sold to the University of West Los Angeles in 2002. Centers were created in Ventura (1991) and Riverside (1992) Counties, and the Athens Center developed into a complete branch campus (1996). The Alaska Center was established in 1970, Taiwan in 1996, and Singapore in 1998.

The mission of the University is to provide "...rich educational opportunities that relate to both the academic and personal development of students." Philosophically, the University emphasizes four major concerns that affirm a positive and rewarding life for its students: personal, professional, and societal values orientation; promoting the goal of community within a context of diversity; lifelong learning; and community service.

The University is comprised of the College of Arts and Sciences, the School of Business and Global Studies, the College of Law, the School of Organizational Management, and the School of Continuing Education . All programs throughout the system are designed, monitored, and controlled through the appropriate departments and colleges at the central campus.

Upon his appointment in 1985, Stephen C. Morgan became the seventeenth president. The longest in tenure, Harold Fasnacht, served twenty years. Morgan's immediate predecessor, Armen Sarafian, had served the University for nine years.

Stephen C. Morgan

Stephen Morgan received a BA in Social Sciences in 1968 from the University of La Verne, a MS in Educational Administration in 1972 from the University of Southern California, and a EdD in Educational Management in 1979 from the University of Northern Colorado.

From 1968 to 1976, he served in a variety of positions at the University of La Verne, including Vice President for Development (1975-76). Subsequently he was Director of Development, University of Southern California (1976-79) and Executive Director, Independent Colleges of Northern California (1979-85).

He has served as a member of the Executive Committee of the Association of Independent California Colleges and Universities and as a member of the Accrediting Commission for Senior Colleges and Universities of the Western Association of Schools and Colleges. He has also served as a Director for the LeRoy Haynes Center, Pomona Valley Hospital Medical Center, the Independent Colleges of Southern California, and the Los Angeles County Fair Association.

Stephen Morgan's comments that follow are a transcript of his interview on August 27, 1999 in his office of the University of La Verne campus. The questions that prompted his comments have either been omitted or are indicated within parentheses.

The Issues and the Turnaround

Well, I wish I had kept a log because I have been here long enough now to every once in a while go through the files and say, oh my, I'd forgotten all about that. I wish that every night or once a week I had written just a little bit about what had transpired that day or week.

When I came to La Verne, it could best be described as an institution that was rudderless. They had had a president who was a graduate of the institution and had been very successful as President of Pasadena City College; he had been here for about seven years. They had consistently run deficits; they had spent down and borrowed from their endowment so they had less than a million dollars invested; they kept extending their line of credit to operate. They literally kept track of how much cash was in the till each month in order to make payroll. There are stories that when people got their paychecks, they rushed to the bank hoping they would be the first wave to deposit their checks. There were months when they borrowed from members of the Board of Trustees on a short-term basis - a hundred thousand here and a hundred thousand there to meet payroll, hopefully having some revenue in the next thirty days to pay off those trustees. They were really very much a hand-to-mouth operation.

We had no endowment. We had no cash - and actually a short-term debt of about $5 million - and had run deficits for a number of years. They would have stacks of checks or accounts payable in the desk drawer of the vice president for finance; he would dole those out when there was money available to cover them. We were on C.O.D. with many vendors and were very deeply in debt with other vendors such as food service and those who had to continue to perform for us because they were really in too far to be able to walk away from us. It was a pretty serious situation.

During the first week as President, I had a meeting with our bankers who were trying to decide what to do with us. I talked fast and furiously about plans and steps I planned to take immediately to turn us around; and I begged for a larger line of credit and more time. Fortunately, they didn't want to foreclose on a university, so they were sympathetic and gave us some breathing room.

My first observation was that we were an institution not living within our means and that the first thing I had to do was pull expenditures into range with revenues. We began to do just that. I figured we were between $500,000 and $750,000 a year out of whack in terms of expenditures over revenues.

We appointed what we called an Options Committee whose charge was to figure out ways to reduce expenditures and/or to increase revenues to close that gap. The group worked from late spring - I had come here in February - and over the first summer in full-day sessions. The Committee included top level administrators, several key faculty members, and several trustees. They gave a lot of time to the effort going through the institution with a fine tooth comb and developed plans for reducing expenditures and increasing revenues. We went without salary increases, didn't fill positions that came open, and looked at new marketing techniques to attract additional students to programs. We introduced this to the University community in September when the faculty returned. We put it into effect and really started working in all areas of marketing and recruitment. Fortunately, for expenditure reduction, we really did not have to make dramatic cuts; we were able to do a lot through attrition and slowing down the rate of expenditure on other than personnel.

The physical plant was a disaster. My wife, who had been a school teacher for a number of years, decided when we moved to La Verne that she didn't want to continue teaching, so I recruited her as an unpaid employee. Her assignment was to do everything she could do to beautify the campus to make it more attractive. I remember we didn't have enough money to paint the inside or outside of buildings, so I said let's make our first effort to at least make sure that wherever we have grass that it is green, and then let's begin to go from there. Fortunately we received a bequest of about $600,000 and that primed the pump to begin campus beautification. We weren't attractive to students or employees, but particularly to prospective students. Other schools in the area were building and beautifying their campuses while La Verne was not a very attractive campus. I felt we just had to move in some of the key areas to make it more attractive so that when we brought students in, they would see a place where they would like to be.

I can also remember one of our key trustees coming in within the first nine or twelve months that I was here. She had been on the Board for a number of years. I just happened to be sitting in my office at lunch time when she came in, huffing and puffing from having come up the stairs. She said she had been on her way to Pomona College, which was her *alma mater*, to offer them a gift of $300,000 but thought they don't need $300,000 and La Verne does. That just made my day - she wrote out a check.

So, the tide began to turn. As I looked at it then and look at it now, it really was a ship without a rudder, without a plan. People were moving in every direction looking for the panacea. Probably the reason I was hired is that I came out of fundraising, and I am sure that the Board saw that as a panacea to cure all of their ills. I knew it wasn't, but I wanted the job badly enough that I wasn't about to tell them that wasn't what I had in mind.

After going through the exercise with the Options Committee and determining how to stop the financial hemorrhaging, we immediately set out on developing a strategic plan - Where do we want to go? Whom do we want to serve? How do we want to serve them?

In undertaking strategic planning, we did it in house. The first time we had one of our faculty members, who was very good in strategic planning, lead the process. The second time, the then Assistant to the President led the process. We looked at outsiders but decided we had what we needed inside. We do use consultants, of course, and I always look for independent ones rather than those who work for large organizations - low overhead consultants who avoid the boiler plate and really get in and learn about the institution. Faculty bought into the strategic planning because they could see it was going to lead somewhere. We also had students involved in both strategic planning processes.

We have gone through two strategic planning processes, and we have really looked at whom we serve. Fortunately, we have reaffirmed that we are not nor should we be a highly selective institution. We serve a need for the student who has potential and has demonstrated ability in high school but who won't be selected by highly selective institutions but who has a lot of potential to be successful. That has helped. Fortunately, not only are we satisfied with that, we are proud of how we address that as an institution. I have watched other institutions try to become highly selective, but I believe there is only so much room for highly selective institutions, and most of them are already there. Very seldom do you see an institution take a quantum leap from being less to highly selective. I think this has been good for us.

There was a negative public image of the University when I arrived. It had been in trouble with WASC [Western Association of Schools and Colleges], and that hit the press. Also there had been numerous articles about the financial condition. When I came, a writer for the *Los Angeles Times* came out to do an interview with me, and I learned a lesson early. The headline ended up being something like 'Small College Attempts to Survive Under Dark Cloud.' It was all about how bad the finances were. I learned then that it takes years and years to turn the image around. I remember going to my ophthalmologist five or six years later. "Oh, you are the President of the University of La Verne. Are they still having all those financial problems?" I realized then how long an image stays in the public's mind. I think we have turned that corner now, and most people look at us as a successful institution. That hurt for a long time. I can remember going into foundations and really having to go through all the financial reports and audits to convince them that we were well managed, well run, and spending our money wisely. So, there was a lot of caution, and a lot of people who said I am not about to give money to you because that would be like putting money down a rat hole.

This negative publicity also had a negative effect on enrollment since we are a regional university and draw heavily from this area.

[*What about your Centers?*] In 1968, Harold Fasnacht, who had been President at La Verne for twenty years retired. Harold had really legitimized La Verne, I like to say. It was the post-war years, and everyone was growing. The veterans came back with money to go into higher education, and foundations were beginning to give money to institutions. So Harold built a physical plant, most of the buildings now on campus, and we were first accredited by WASC during that time. We became a member of the Independent Colleges of Southern California. Harold really went out and took this little institution that had struggled for years and years and tried to solidify it by making it legitimate.

In 1969, Lee Newcomer, an innovative educator and graduate of La Verne, became President. He is the one who said I am not a good fundraiser and won't be very successful building the endowment, but I will create a living endowment by opening markets and providing education for adult students that will be profitable to the institution. So where you spend a dollar and a quarter for each dollar you take in for a traditional undergraduate student, I'll develop an off-campus program in which for every dollar taken in, we would only spend seventy or seventy-five cents. That will help balance the budget. Lee took that on, and we went for a wild ride. We went all across the United States, offering units for most anything, working with lots of subcontractors.

Well, Kay Anderson [then Executive Director of WASC's Commission on Senior Colleges and Universities] really clamped down on that quickly so that we were in big trouble with accreditation. This struggle continued for a number of years. Over time, I think the University was successful in convincing WASC that we were offering quality and that we were putting quality controls in place. When WASC came in 1980 or 1981, not only did they see this empire off campus, they also saw the severe financial problems. I think they put the institution on Show Cause [*i.e.,* why accreditation should not be removed] for a period of time, and we pulled it out.

But, when I came we still had this on-going battle with WASC.

[*What is the financial situation now?*] Today, we have $30 million in endowment and about $15 million in planned gifts that will eventually be added to the endowment. We had a record fundraising effort this past - over $7 million, including planned gifts. We ended the past year with about a $2.5 million surplus out of a $58-$60 million budget. We closed the last 13 years with a surplus and put about $12 to $15 million into campus improvements and have plans to continue doing that. We borrowed through tax-exempt bonds to do a lot of the work. We are still tuition-dependent and have record numbers of students coming in this year. We are experiencing the benefits of the new generation of students in California.

[*Academic Programs?*] Actually it was our academic vice president, who came after I arrived, who really started to put in a quality assurance program by getting on-campus, full-time faculty involved with the off-campus programs, the review of part-time faculty credentials and performance, and review of all curricula. Today, all programs that are offered off-campus are the same programs offered on-campus; we don't offer anything off-campus that we do not have a base for on-campus. It is the on-campus departments and schools that are in charge of the curriculum wherever it is delivered by the University. Serious control measures are in place. In consequence we have been in a much stronger position with WASC, and they have looked at us as a legitimate institution offering programs off-campus.

We operate in professional development centers here in Southern California - we have one in Orange County, one in Ventura County, in Burbank, and Rancho Cucamonga. Usually we are in commercial buildings with classrooms, computer labs, and small libraries with access to Wilson Library on campus. We also operate clusters throughout the State of California in a variety of locations and are on some military bases here in California, and we have several small programs in Alaska. And, we do have a branch campus in Athens, Greece that has grown to nine hundred students with its own full-time faculty. It started on a military base and grew slowly. Then we realized there was a need for programs for civilians. At that time, non-

Greek citizens could not attend Greek universities. So that program grew and grew. Now there is no longer a military base, but our program continues. It is a kind of wholly-owned subsidiary incorporated under Greek law as a Greek corporation; it has its own president who reports to the University. That program has been quite successful although it doesn't provide a lot of financial support for us. When we are accredited, some of the members of the visiting team get to go to Athens to that campus to review it.

The off-campus programs are about 60 percent of our enrollment; 80 percent of our students are over the age of twenty-five, only 20 percent are traditional age. The off-campus programs have been important for us because we have been able to keep them profitable while also maintaining quality. But, obviously, they don't require the services and facilities of a traditional undergraduate institution.

Nonetheless, we are encountering increased competition in all of our adult programs not only with the Phoenixes but also our sister institutions - Pepperdine and Redlands are all in that market. When we started in that market thirty years ago, we were pioneers, and people looked down their noses at us. Now when I look through the *LA Times,* I see ads for UCLA [University of California - Los Angeles], USC [University of Southern California], and Claremont Graduate University for adult programs. We have decided it is a niche that is important to us and have reaffirmed our commitment to the adult market both on and off the campus. But, we can never take our eye off the compass.

I think there is a window of opportunity over the next five to eight years to have some enrollment growth if the economy stays strong and fundraising remains good. People have more wealth than they ever dreamed they would have given the stock market over the last five or six years. Lots of good things have happened, but I don't sleep through every night when I start to think about the things that could go wrong. You can never take your eye off the management side of it.

Looking over the years at our enrollment, I am pleased that we are a diversified institution because there have been times when our traditional undergraduate enrollment was dipping but the adult population was growing, and vice versa. That has been good for us not to have all of our eggs in one basket.

[*The Board?*] I have had a very supportive Board of Trustees; they have been with me. I work hard to make sure that they know what's going on; I keep them well-informed. If I have a proposal for them, we have thought about it carefully, spending a lot of time presupposing what their questions might be. It is not a terribly wealthy Board although we are slowly attempting to change that and bring on people who have more personal wealth. But, they have been very supportive and that has been helpful. I would never have lasted this long if they had not been as supportive as they are.

[*Morale?*] When I arrived, morale in the faculty was low but hopeful. I think there is always an energy that comes with new leadership. Even if you have a strong leader, I think there is always a hopefulness when a new leader comes into an institution. Fortunately, we began to see results fairly fast, and part of that is just luck. I often say when you look at successful or less than successful presidents of the United States, it's mostly an effect of what the economy was when they are in office. If it isn't doing well, they are not reelected, and if it is, they are.

Part of what happened here was good fortune and good luck, but part of it was hard work and strategic at the same time. The hopeful morale at the time quickly rose as the fortunes of the institution grew. Now the expectations are higher, and we may have more difficulty at times managing morale today than we did then. In those early years, people could say look how much progress we've made and remember how bad it was. Now there are fewer who remember how bad it was, so the expectations are higher. So we have had some interesting morale dilemmas recently over issues like faculty salaries and their comparisons with other schools. We are still not a wealthy institution.

The academic governance structure that was in place when I arrived has been changed dramatically. The academic vice president, who came shortly after I did, really worked to build a new faculty governance system. This past year, the faculty wanted to have a senate, not having had one previously. You know, everyone has a senate, and now we have one, too. That is partly my own fault; I didn't stay close enough to the faculty, and some of the academic administrators weren't staying close enough to the faculty either. So a communications gap developed. Fortunately, the people who formed the Senate really wanted to close that communications gap in a positive way. It has worked out very well. It was a wake-up call to remind us that we really have to stay in touch with the faculty. They need to be involved. They were involved in all University committees, but there were some upper-level decisions made in which they were not included.

We have a very diverse student body, particularly among our undergraduates: 30 percent Latino, 10 percent African-American, 7 or 8 percent Asian. What we saw was that we were being very successful with first generation students and with this very diverse student body. So we decided to work harder to build the student body along those diverse lines. We also saw that we were very successful with the student who comes in with a three point, give or take, grade point average and a thousand or so on the SAT. We decided that was a niche we wanted to go for but to shape it so that there were fewer at the lower end of the spectrum, and that is exactly what we are doing. But it was just two years ago that we reorganized the admissions process and the way we award financial aid to really focus on those kinds of students in a strategic way.

Attrition has been a matter of concern and still is. We have a pretty mobile student body, but it has improved dramatically.

We are also planning for growth of the traditional undergraduate program - we have been at about a thousand, give or take a hundred, for years. We are now moving toward a traditional undergraduate enrollment of about thirteen or fourteen hundred and want to increase our facilities. There are some economies of scale we can achieve by doing that.

The community of La Verne is not especially wealthy. It is basically a bedroom community. There is probably more wealth now with some high end homes that have been built in the last five to ten years north of La Verne, but those people have no allegiance to the University. We have never been a wealthy institution. We were founded by the Church of the Brethren, a small, not wealthy denomination, but we were never heavily supported by the Church although by some Church members over the years. We have trained a lot of very successful school teachers, but they are not wealthy, and we have not attracted wealthy students. We have an ongoing effort to build the board with members who have some wealth. We have also worked hard to recruit local students who come from wealthier families to develop some alumni who have some wealth. We have done well with California foundations on special projects such as the Irvine Foundation on issues of first generation students and helping with issues of diversity and supporting the needs of a diverse student body.

We have a very good working relationship with the City of La Verne, and I try to open the doors whenever there is a need we can meet in terms of facilities. If we have special events on campus, we also open our doors. We have good relationships with the City - the City Manager and Assistant City Manager are graduates of La Verne, and two of the Council members work for the University. As result, we have a very positive partnership with them, and they have worked hard to try to maintain a balance with the University and the downtown area.

Like most communities, there are a lot of newcomers who do not have much loyalty to the City of La Verne or the University. The Church of the Brethren, which was founded about the same time as the University in 1891, came to La Verne, and for years it was the dominating church. A lot of the leadership on the City Council came out of the Church of the Brethren. That has really changed dramatically to a much more ecumenical and diverse community than it was at that time.

We have had a College of Law for twenty-seven years, and we have decided to make an effort to position it for ABA [American Bar Association] accreditation. We have been very successful; we have been California Bar accredited, and, as we speak, we are negotiating with the City of Ontario for a 60,000 square foot building they have near the City Hall along with some cash to go with that. We will need to put about $4 million into the building to remodel and restore it. Hopefully then we will be within twelve to twenty-four months of applying for ABA approval. We think that would be a quantum leap in the prestige of the University. [Ed. Note: ABA accreditation was granted in Spring 2006.]

We have also just brought together all of our Education programs; we have been very successful in training administrators and teachers. Our EdD program is second only to USC [University of Southern California] in the number of graduates who are superintendents in California. We really have a fine reputation in training teachers and administrators. We have brought all those programs under one umbrella, are forming a School of Education, and are now searching for a dean. We really looked at what we are best known for and kept coming back to the same answer- we are best known for what we do in Education. So why aren't we building more partnerships, and why don't we try to become a more significant player in California as it looks at how to improve public education? And, as money is focused and also with the need for school teachers in the State, let's try to get as much of that piece as we can.

[*Observations?*] I am more and more convinced that college presidents in tuition-dependent institutions are managers and leaders and that our first responsibility is to make sure we live within our means, realize realistically what revenues are, budget conservatively, help the institution create a vision it can embrace, and enable and empower everyone to move in the same direction.

I've also learned that institutions take sequential steps; very seldom do they take quantum leaps from point A to point D without going through B and C. I realize we take baby steps oftentimes. They have to be sequential, building on what we have done before. Now, looking back over fourteen years, I can see that we have made enormous progress, but it has been one step at a time. A lot of it is common sense to me. It is amazing, as I look at other institutions, how frequently top leadership isn't leading with common sense.

We had budgeted very unrealistically over the years. They would get into budget sessions and be a million dollars short so they would say, we will just increase fundraising. We'll just plug in that figure in spite of the fact that no fundraising at La Verne had ever been that successful. So they counted on pennies from heaven - or dollars. There were some people who made some very large gifts during that time being told if you give us a half million dollars, we can pay our bills, prime the pump and get us started--and three months later the University would be right back where it was before.

Being an experienced fundraiser, I knew that wasn't the way it worked and that it would take time to build. It is logical, sequential to build consensus on campus on the direction we want to go, how we want to do it, budgeting conservatively and realistically. I planned for surpluses every year, and faculty would have screamed had they known we had that much money they would have asked for more salary. But I knew they had insatiable appetites and that we would never be able to fulfill their desires. Then we had money at the end of the year to put into the plant fund or to help build the quasi-endowment.

As you know, in higher education, everything is measured by inputs and as a tuition-driven, not very wealthy, institution, our inputs don't compare with a Pomona or a Claremont- McKenna in whose shadow we live. We have never done a very good job of measuring what we actually do for our students. That is why I'm supportive of the new WASC initiatives regarding assessment. I have always suspected that we may make a lot more difference to a student over four years than does a very selective school. If I took in students with nothing but 1300 to 1600 SATS and 4.0s, how could I not be successful with them? But, if you bring in a student with a 2.7, a 900 SAT who is first generation from central Los Angeles, and he or she graduates with a bachelor's degree, gets a teaching credential, and becomes a very successful school principal - we may have made more of a difference. But we don't measure that well, and we don't articulate it. So the *U.S. News and World Report* still prevails - and we are never very high in it!

I kid my friends at the Claremont Colleges by saying, "If you brought those kids together and didn't have any faculty at all, they would come out of your institution as very bright, capable kids. So be careful and don't screw them up."

I have a real missionary zeal for what places like La Verne do with the students we serve, and that is what keeps me going. I really believe that higher education in Southern California can be the most effective vehicle to bring the diversity that it has together for common purposes. We can do more to level the playing field through education than through any other vehicle.

I believe that most presidents go into their jobs with their eyes open and know what the issues are. But, until you sit in the chair and the bombs keep dropping on you day after day after day, you can't imagine what it is like. I guess what probably was the real surprise was the reality of it all. It was as bad as I thought it was, and suddenly when you are the one responsible for trying to turn the tide, it impacts you very differently.

Would You Do It Again?

Yes, and I would like to add to the story. I had worked here, I'm a third generation graduate of La Verne, and I knew how bad it was, but I really wanted to be a college president. I thought if I ever had a shot at it, it would be my *alma mater*. The Board went through a search process and got down to three finalists, including me. As the Search Committee started narrowing it down, one of the finalists dropped out - he got another presidency. So they were down to two. The other had been a successful president someplace else, so they decided to go with him because he had a track record, and I didn't. One of the members of the Search Committee happened to be a personnel guy from a school district, and he said. "We've checked all of Steve's credentials, and we know they are okay because he got some of them here, and we know his history. Has anyone checked the other candidate's credentials?" "Well, he has a doctorate from Columbia." This fellow said, "Do you know that?" "Well, it's on his resume. But, you may want to check." Well, they did check and found he had a store-bought degree from a store-front place called Columbia. Then, they were in a real dilemma - they felt he had been dishonest and could not go with him. They were under a lot of pressure to find a president so they really took me without having another choice; they took the risk. I can tell that story now.

Neil J. Hoffman, Otis College of Art and Design

The Institution

Otis College of Art and Design, founded in 1918, is an independent non-profit visual arts institution (Specialized - Art) with locations in the California Mart in the City of Los Angeles and the West Side Campus in Westchester, California and an enrollment of about 1,000, with students from all fifty states and more than thirty foreign countries.

At its founding as Otis Art Institute, it was housed in a Spanish-Moorish mansion that had been bequeathed to the City of Los Angeles by General Harrison Gray Otis, the founder and publisher of the *Los Angeles Times*. Students were called 'Otisians,' and the school was affectionately called 'The Bivouc,' General Otis' name for his home. During the 1940s, Norman Rockwell was artist-in-residence, sometimes using students for his *Saturday Evening Post* covers. In 1949, the Institute was renamed Los Angeles County Art Institute, and in 1954 it became a four year college offering both Bachelor's and Master's degrees in Fine Arts. It reassumed its original name in 1960. In 1979, the College merged with the New School for Social Research in New York and became part of a three school consortium with Parsons School of Design in New York and Paris; at that time it was renamed Otis Art Institute of Parsons School of Design. That merger dissolved in 1991. The Institute's name was then changed to Otis College of Art and Design to reflect the broader curricular divisions of the institution, the School of Fashion Design having been founded in 1980. In 1992, its status was changed to an independent, non-profit college.

The mission of the College is "...a community committed to integrating visual and critical thinking to educate future professionals."

The first year, for all students, is called Foundation Year in which fundamental activities of art making (studio classes in life drawing, drawing and composition, color and design, and form and space) are combined with core studies in the liberal arts and sciences to provide the basic skills and visual language necessary to succeed in any major. The purpose of Foundation Year is to enable would-be artists or designers to analyze the social and cultural environment in which they live, to critically evaluate the impact it has on them, and to effect changes on society as well as to examine more closely each discipline and department of the College.

Upon his initial appointment in 1979, Neil Hoffman became Dean and Chief Executive Officer, the longest in tenure in that role having been Millard Sheets who served eight years. When he returned in 1993, Hoffman became the second president, his immediate predecessor, Roger Workman, having served in that role for two years. Hoffman retired in June, 2000, then served as Associate Director of the WASC Commission on Senior Colleges and Universities (2005-2007) until assuming the position of President of the Milwaukee Institute of Art and Design in July, 2007.

Neil J. Hoffman

Neil Hoffman received a BS in Art Education (Studio Major: Painting) in 1960 and a MS in Art Education (Studio Major: Photography) in 1967 from SUNY Buffalo. From 1968-73, he undertook post-graduate course work at SUNY-Brockport in Administration of Higher Education and at Niagara University in Curriculum Development and Supervision.

His teaching experience included: Art Teacher at Huth Road Elementary School (1961-64) and Grand Island Jr.-Sr. High School (1965-69); Professor and Chairman of the First Year Basic Arts Program (1969-71) and graduate school instructor for preparation of college professors (FIPSE funded) (1971-74), College of Fine and Applied Art, Rochester Institute of Technology; Instructor in Art, Boston University (1974-79); and Lecturer at Otis College of Art and Design, California College of Arts and Crafts, Art Institute of Chicago, and Otis Art Institute of Parsons

School of Design (1979-97).

Hoffman's administrative experience included: Chairman, Unified Arts Department, Grand Island Public Schools (NY) (1968-69); Assistant Dean (1969-72) and Associate Dean-Associate Professor, College of Fine and Applied Art, Rochester Institute of Technology (1969-74); Founding Director, Program in Artisanry, Boston University (1974-79); Founding Dean/Chief Administrative Officer, Otis Art Institute of Parsons School of Design (1979-83); President, School of the Art Institute of Chicago (1983-85); and President, California College of Arts and Crafts (1985-93).

In addition to remaining active as a professional photographer, including an exhibit at the Albright Knox Gallery in Buffalo, he has served on accreditation teams of the Western Association of Schools and Colleges, in leadership roles in the National Association of Art and Design, on the American Film Institute's Advisory Committee, on the Executive Committee of the Association of Independent California Colleges and Universities, and as Vice President of the Alliance of Independent Colleges of Arts, among other professional activities. Community service has included being a regional member of the Los Angeles Cultural Affairs Department, member of the Directors of the LAX/Westchester Chamber of Commerce, on the advisory panel for the California Arts Council, and Chairman of the City of Oakland's Cultural Planning Process.

Among his professional honors are: Commendation for Contribution to the Arts of Los Angeles County from the Los Angeles Board of Supervisors (1983); Illinois Art Education Association Award (1985); SUNY Buffalo Alumni of the Year (1986); Oakland Business Arts Award for community leadership (1991); and Selection Committee, Governor's Arts Awards (1991).

Neil Hoffman's comments that follow are a transcript of his interview on August 26, 1999 in his office at the Otis College of Art and Design. The questions that prompted his comments have either been omitted or are indicated within parentheses.

146

The Issues and the Turnaround

When I arrived at Otis in 1993 for the second time, I found what was characteristic of struggling institutions. First, there was a lack of vision and mission and hence a lack of planning coupled with no leadership. In the absence of not knowing where the place was going and not having a road map to get there, the recruiting effort had been affected resulting in unstable and unpredictable enrollments. Since Otis is tuition-dependent, there was a financial problem. The final result was the negative impact on institutional climate. [Ed. note: This paragraph is a paraphrase of Hoffman's complete statement, which is found beginning on page 4]

Fortunately, Otis had a core of very good, loyal faculty - otherwise this would not have been of interest to me - and a core group of dedicated trustees, but overall, it didn't know how to get out of the pickle. The reason should be obvious in that they were first publicly supported or supported by another institution (Parsons) that provided the financing and infrastructure - it was a division of something else. Upon becoming an independent college, it was fraught with weaknesses.

Prior to my arrival, the Board had just fired the President, WASC accreditation was very critical, the endowment was $300,000, and enrollment was flat because of the location of the campus, [adjacent to MacArthur Park, then a high crime area, in downtown Los Angeles], creating a 36 percent annual attrition rate.

The first thing I did would probably sound crazy to the average administrator - we began long-range planning in my first month. The reason was the lack of vision and poor institutional climate.

I did not learn planning strategies and governance processes in a college or as an administrator. I learned them as the chair of the cultural planning process for the City of Oakland. I learned by working with a professional facilitator and assuming a position that we were going to be inclusive rather than exclusive. We began by identifying the individuals who represented the cultural interests of the City and those who enjoyed the most respect. We asked them to participate. We started identifying the strengths and weaknesses of the cultural life of the City and translating them into a set of shared goals, seven or eight of them. The process not only created goals, it brought the community together. It included not only the providers but also the sponsors, the corporations - all in the same room dreaming and defining the future. I've been using that approach in colleges now for twelve years.

I believe very strongly that the final planning document really doesn't matter. What is important is the shared vision and values. This necessitates that long-range planning be on-going. If people believe in it, it's theirs. Frankly, the way I view it, the process is the product. It is not about a document or even an action plan. It's about people buying into and believing in something.

When an institution is struggling and the faculty and staff feel as if their jobs are jeopardized, they transfer it to the students. That doesn't mean they get out on a soapbox and say 'We're in trouble' - it is more subtle. For example, if a student has trouble registering, is mad about it, and says that the place is messed up, the teacher doesn't disagree. She looks to the sky in resignation as opposed to a response in which the teacher says, you go to Ed, he will take care of it. In other words they take pride in their school.

Some years ago, I recall being concerned that subordinates were outguessing me or concealing good ideas because I was the boss. So, I went to an outside consultant who interviewed fifty people regarding my performance. They basically took me apart. Then I attended a retreat with four other CEOS of for-profit institutions. The consultants took us apart in front of each other and analyzed our strengths and weaknesses. It was a mind-boggling experience. One of my weaknesses was the lack of long-range planning! That was a turning point; I didn't realize I was operating on intuition. That, coupled with the experience in cultural planning led me to reinvent myself - which is probably what happens all the time if you want to grow and keep your job interesting.

In addition to initiating long-range planning, some additional changes were implemented. An enrollment management approach as opposed to an admissions office approach means examining everything from inquiry generation, catalogs, and publications to the involvement of alumni, everything from recruitment to retention being viewed as a continuum. One of the goals of this view of enrollment management is that everyone feels as if they have a shared relationship with the lives of those students. No one is doing anything bad; it is that everyone must think about the experience from the vantage point of the student.

The faculty accepted their role in this concept. They were so ready, because it was so frustrating to spend all your time grumbling. Bosses often say employees grumble all the time. The truth is they don't want to. If there is a large group of people that are grumbling all the time, you are not doing your job right and not providing leadership. My view of leadership in today's culture is not telling people what to do but empowering and respecting them to define their own jobs to meet the shared goals.

One of the tricks that illustrates this, and which I tried a number of years ago, is that I walked into a room where all of the heads of the different departments were gathered. I then went around the room to each of the supervisors and said that I was going to tell them something that needed improvement in each of the departments based on my first month's observations. I said to the registrar that if he wanted to accurately reflect what it feels like to be a student at registration, you should play cattle sounds out there because people are lined up in a sweaty room waiting patiently for hours. I went around the room and told each something very simple so they knew that I knew something about their job. I didn't cast it by saying they were doing bad things nor anything that could be taken personally. I said that the first half of your job is to learn to be a manager - that we can teach you. The second half, and the most important part of the job, is creative thinking - how to do something different and better, an idea invented by yourself.

I said that every Monday we are going to meet, and next Monday I want you to come into the room with two creative ideas to improve the quality of service to students, be more efficient, and improve conversion rates. It will be measured ultimately by enrollment outcomes. So bring your ideas, I don't care how crazy they are - just something that you think could make a difference. You can talk with students and colleagues for their input.

So, they came in the next week, and each of them had two ideas. Everyone of them were good ideas because it released their pent-up frustrations. The trick is, like Mark Twain, I was empowering them to paint the fence. They had come up with twenty-two creative ideas, and they were all set to leave the room because the hour was up, and I asked with whom we had to consult to implement these twenty-two ideas. Is there anyone negatively impacted or whose opinion we need or someone who might be an obstacle? They agreed no, so I said, implement all these ideas by next week and come in with two more. They did this for six months, and the total cost was $380 for an idea that came from the buildings and grounds supervisor who said, 'We have this beautiful outside patio, and we have chairs and nice gardens; if we just built a redwood seat around the garden, kids could sit next to the garden and have this nice view, and I'll build it.'

These were empowered people who had become part of changing the climate, doing it in a responsible way. Seems pretty simple to me, and it worked.

It's a long time since I let go of the commanding and control approach. It's like the business of fundraising - the donor is actually your friend, it's not a fake thing. You have to believe in other people and their abilities because, collectively, they are going to do more than you could ever imagine, and they are going to like it better.

When I came on board, the endowment was $300,000. Seven years later, with the completion of a challenge match, the endowment will be $6 million. We have also raised $14 million toward a $16 million capital campaign. The remaining balance is $1 million for the new building and the other $1 million is part of a challenge match for endowment. We are about twelve months away. This is quite an accomplishment for an institution that in 1979 had annual fundraising of $50,000, which was attributed to an annual scholarship dinner that cost the institution $20,000!

Although not cost effective, it was important because the people who were there were genuine and very important to the institution. The organization that created that is still with us and functioning on its own and donating between $25,000 and $50,000 in scholarships each year, which really affects our students' lives.

Members of the Board have played an active role in the person-to-person solicitation for funds. I do not know of any private college in which the Board members are not central to the fundraising effort. Usually, the more responsibility one has on the Board, the more the community looks to that person to lead by example. While it may not always be the biggest check, often the person who is in that position is there because they want to lead, to set an example. Also, it is very difficult for a Board member to ask someone else who has the same financial capability for a gift larger than they gave. Joe, would you give me a million dollars, and Joe asks how much have you given - a half million? - okay I'll give you half a million or a quarter of a million.

As I mentioned earlier, there was no faculty governance. But, then the College was very small in 1979 and didn't need much in the way of faculty governance. I certainly knew that over the history of the institution some wonderful things happened without a formal faculty process. It probably was more like an artists' colony or artists' group that worked together depending on whether the president was a benevolent dictator or a cooperative, participatory type of person.

When I came in 1979, the faculty had been very influential in the late 1970s in creating the three school consortium. They chose the school to be affiliated with. They were delighted with their power, influence, and decision. But shortly after the decision was made, in comes a new dean and CEO - me - and the anxieties they had before did not just go away. They prevailed. I tried to beat it to death with talking and communicating and being on campus. It was a slow, arduous task and took about a year. The faculty group was meeting in secret, and I wasn't invited to participate. What they would do is share the most recent rumors until finally one of the faculty stood up and said, 'Do you see any blood around here, did you see anyone die, lose their jobs? Why don't we give everybody a break and let's go forward.' They all agreed, 'What are we worrying about?'

With that in my mind and my other experience, when I returned to Otis this time, I realized that creating a governance system and planning process needed to be done at the same time. I went to the first faculty planning meetings where they sat there one night until ten o'clock trying to figure out how to organize the faculty into a governance structure. At one point, someone said, 'Neil will tell us what to do.' Someone else said, 'But, he's the boss.' I didn't rise to the bait and said I believed a governance structure had to be created by them.

Experience tells me that when you do that, they come to you for advice, not to be told what to do. And so, over the course of one year, it evolved - I directed them to five schools that had good models. One of the models was the Art Institute of Chicago, where the governance structure was extremely good and made it very easy for me to work with them during my short stay there. The model we ended up with here was similar to theirs. However, when it was done, it was their investment.

After the first year, we had a fall-to-fall attrition rate of 36 percent; the second year, it went to 27 percent, the third year to 22 percent, and in 1999, it was under 15 percent. And, the institution has never been as selective as it is now: thirty thousand inquiries, fifteen hundred applications, and three hundred new students. We raised standards to meet our goals. One of the myths of enrollment management is that you get more students by lowering your standards. But if you lower your standards and are unsure about your mission, the only students who attend are those who see you as a second or third choice and transfer later. We have a clear shared vision, good planning, clarity of our future, what we stand for, and what we don't.

There is very little crime on the Westchester campus [located on the west side of Los Angeles] in contrast to the previous location near MacArthur Park, where neighborhood crime was all around us. We literally locked ourselves away from it, so we had no environment around the college. Here, we have a very open campus - we have no walls, and people are very comfortable walking out of their rooms and leaving their stuff out all the time. Every once in a while someone will pick something up, so we have to remind them to secure their valuables.

[*Observations?*] My experience with the California College of Arts and Crafts is very similar to what I did here. What I've discovered over the last twenty years is that there are more institutions with ingredients of ailments than those without. One of the examples to illustrate is when I was part of a planning process for one of the WASC [Western Association of Schools and Colleges] Annual Meetings. A group of presidents said let's really do something worthwhile for the other presidents. After a long debate, we decided that we would try to have the stronger, healthier institutions help the struggling ones. To this, the Provost at USC [University of Southern California], Bob Biller, laughed and said that USC was a struggling institution, and I said, you know what I mean. We had quite a bit of banter over that. Finally I decided that we should attempt to define very simply what a struggling institution was, and I suggested it was any college that had less than a million dollars in endowment. I had a gale of laughter to that, and the head of WASC said that 100 of the 147 WASC accredited colleges have less than a million dollar endowment. That is quite a testimony as to how tenuous institutions are when you see that endowments are almost non-existent. Now that ten years have passed, those figures may have changed, but you probably could use that as a level of insight - namely that they are completely tuition dependent.

For the WASC conference, the group decided to help college presidents understand more about fundraising. We had terrific speakers, and I was taking extensive notes even though I had been fundraising for a long time. Each of us who organized the planning exercise chaired discussion groups of similar types of institutions. I started my group of forty with a lead question. The room was dead, there wasn't a sound, no one was talking. So I tried another approach, hoping to liven it up, otherwise we would be sitting there for an hour doing nothing. I asked how many enjoyed fundraising - three hands went up, and one of them was mine. I asked, how many of you would enjoy fundraising if you were good at it. All the hands went up.

It wasn't a matter of whether or not they were being asked to do something they didn't want to, but they didn't know how to do it. I stated that there were ten myths about fundraising . The first is that people give you money because you need it. The second myth is that people give you money because you are good. Third, people give you money because you have written a good proposal. After going through this long list, the heads were turning left and right because they thought they were truths. Someone burst out saying if it wasn't those things then why do people give you money? I said, people give money to people, it's personal, and it's not phony. It's genuine.

I have never had a person make a large gift who was not a friend. Wealthy, smart people give money smart, and they are going to give it where they believe in the leadership, believe in the vision, and have been close long enough to know that the investment is going to do something special for the institution and that it will reflect positively on them. And the naming opportunity is really a source of pride - some ego-satisfaction - but generally a source of pride. So when all these elements are in play, you can't raise money if you don't know where you are going or who is going to do the asking.

One of the best interviews I experienced was with the Provost of the New School for Social Research, Allan Austel. It was an hour I will never forget. He got to the end of it and said, 'Neil I just have one more question.' While looking out the window as if it were just a throw-away question, he said, 'Neil, how do you know when you are doing a good job?' I felt as if I thought about that for five hours, and each time I developed an answer or response, I realized it wasn't right. I finally said, 'When no one notices me.' He did ask another question - 'Are you going to take the job?' The point is that it is not about ego but how you make things work - it's the difference between riding a horse and driving a tank. The tank responds to the lever being pushed down - the horse is a living part of the ride. The horse is not a good metaphor for an educational institution but similarly it is a living entity that has to be nurtured.

I believe in a coordinated approach to management by first learning how to be a manager. As a basic, do you regularly bring in your employees and evaluate them, and what do you base it on? However, if you mark them all fives if the highest is five, you are not doing anyone a favor, and people don't appreciate an arbitrary evaluation. They want a real one. So you are going to have to learn how to do that.

The reason I became an administrator is that I didn't like the way they treated people. I got involved by thinking of ways to involve people and treat them better. It simply evolved over forty years into something. With the faculty there was some nervousness about when the time came to hire a new president. I reminded them that they have a governance structure, know what you expect from leadership, are capable of hiring a president, and have created a climate in which anyone would be lucky to be here.

In my last institution, I did not want a good bye party so they gave me a roast instead. At the end of the program, I said, 'All I did was to direct the institution, you did all the work.'

Would You Do It Over Again?

Yes, my intentions were deliberately progressing from one level to another. I went into teaching for the very same reasons I became a college president - I really wanted my life to make a difference. All you can do is do what you believe in and listen to whether or not it works. And if it doesn't, you have to step back and say I didn't do that right and ask other people for advice - and really listen. After all, we come into this world knowing nothing about it and go out knowing only a little bit more.

We may not, as human beings, be sure of our purpose but surely the search must be in front of you. And you have to be in tune with the qualities in others.

In one job I had, I knew that my leadership was personality-driven, and when I left it ended up in big-time trouble. I didn't want that to happen again. So I have put a lot more effort into thinking about giving other people responsibility, to engender leadership in others resulting in an entire organization rising up beyond individual expectations. I would hope things will be sustained here. It was my goal to change the climate by empowering others. I think that is what everyone expects. And although personal styles differ, the person who comes in here is going to have to have a philosophical basis that is in tune with an organization that is used to working together. So I am not worried about it.

The decision to move to this campus and the eight major goals we created in 1993 have all been implemented with no dissenting votes, because no one was voting. This is not about democracy but about forging a vision and implementing and assuming your own role in it. In Faculty Senate meetings, they seldom vote. If they can't resolve an issue, they will have members go off and work on the problems until they are resolved - they hammer it out until it works. This minimizes the politics, which are too much a part of higher education.

Part Three: Analysis of the Nine Presidential Stories

Introduction

The stories of the nine presidents are, in effect, case studies, and, as such, need to be analyzed by way of a theoretical framework to provide coherency and organization. To that end, we have selected the four frames theory advanced by Bolman and Deal (1997) for several reasons: it provides a useful and easily accessible framework to elicit commonalities and differences among the strategies employed by the nine presidents; it is a well-known theoretical framework for analysis of organizational change; it provides an adaptable lens for looking at the mass of information in the case studies to ascertain why these presidents made a difference and why they were successful salvaging presidents in reframing their institution; and, finally, it is used in many higher education courses on organizing and foundational leadership theory.

Parenthetically, it is to be noted that in their 1997 publication, Bolman and Deal present very few instances or examples of their theoretical framework in higher education. We are hopeful that our analyses, using their framework, will add to the limited theoretical literature on salvaging presidents.

For those readers who may not be familiar with, or need a reminder about, the four-frame model of the Bolman and Deal theory, a brief recapitulation in their language is in order.

The four-frame model views organizations metaphorically as factories, families, jungles, and temples when seen from the frames, respectively, of structure, human resources, politics, and symbols. The *structural frame* emphasizes goals, specialized roles, and formal relationships (*e.g,* the organizational chart) that fit an organization's environment and technology; there is allocation of responsibilities, rules, policies, and procedures to coordinate diverse activities. The *human resource frame* focuses on the relationship between the organization and people, who are seen, metaphorically, like an extended family of individuals who have needs, feelings, prejudices, skills, and limitations, all of which are challenges to finding ways to get the job(s) done with the people feeling good about what they are doing. The *political frame* sees organizations as arenas in which different interests compete for power and scarce resources, and wherein bargaining, negotiation, coercion, and compromise are part of everyday life; problems arise if power is concentrated in the wrong places or is so broadly dispersed that nothing gets done; solutions arise from political skill and acumen. The *symbolic frame* sees organizations as cultures propelled more by rituals, ceremonies, stories, heroes, and myths than by rules, policies, and managerial authority; this frame also sees organizations as a theater in which actors play their roles, poorly or well, in the organizational drama; problems arise when symbols lose their meaning and ceremonies and rituals lose their potency.

In the analysis that follows, the various strategies and actions the presidents employed are included under the respective frame in the following order - structural, human resource, political, and symbolic. In some instances, a given strategy or action may well fall under more than one frame given its particular conditions. In all cases, the number(s) in parentheses following a strategy or action refers to the page in the interview where the fuller description can be found. A reader may disagree with some of our categorizations, believing a different or more than one placement would be more appropriate. Please be our guest.

The Analyses

Dr. Donald Averill and Palo Verde College

Averill's introduction of Board training to enable members to understand their proper role and responsibilities (18) ("...the Board was materially involved in micromanaging the District") is one instance of employing the structural frame as was his decision to adhere to the law with regard to offering public safety programs in which the College did the teaching, not the agencies, and thereby properly collected the apportionment money (20). Further, the development of working relationships with four-year California State University (CSU)-Chico and CSU-San Bernardino to offer teacher education programs in that underserved area (21) and reinstituting programs for the employees of the Chuckawall Prison as well as the farming community (22) were basic structural strategies. The strategy of a weekly letter to the Board informing them of whatever was happening (18) precluded the untoward consequences of surprises.

Falling under the human resources frame were his resolving, by direct intervention, the several litigation issues that had been festering for years (17), attention to due process (17), the decision to terminate no employees or seek the resignation of any Board member (17) ("I decided not to fire anybody and, instead, try to work things out"), providing continuing opportunities for Board training (18-19), and a willingness to listen to and address faculty concerns (19).

Averill's political skills and acumen were evident in the development of community support for the College (19-20), re-instituting non-credit courses of interest to the local community (21), the development with the City of Blythe and other entities of an aggressive economic diversity development plan that led to the establishment of a Small Business Development Center and an "Empowerment Zone" (22-23), his presidency of the local Chamber of Commerce (24), reestablishing ties with the Community Colleges Chancellor's Office (27), working around the faculty's stonewalling leadership to get moving on contract negotiations (26), and his adroit use of what he termed 'canal diplomacy' to turn people around (17, 24).

His leadership in getting faculty and recalcitrant Board members focused on the future in the Future Research project (24) and developing an appropriate model for program review (24) were tangible instances of using symbolic reframing.

Dr. Thomas E. J. DeWitt and Lasell College

deWitt's getting staff trained in operations management (34), remaking the College from a two-year to a four-year institution (34, 49-50) and then to co-educational (39-42, 43-44), building a business climate and retrofitting a business center into a teaching day-care center (35), providing monthly information to the Board (35-36), investing in technology and facilities (38), and constructing the design of Lasell Village (48-49) may all be viewed as a structural reframing of Lasell College.

Very conscious of his human resources, deWitt endeavored to "get everybody on board" (35-36), educated, developed, and empowered the Board (36, 44-47), rehired (36-37) and empowered (43) faculty ("...I needed their good will in order to go four-year"), built a strong and independent administrative team (37-38), developed new procedures for evaluation of the president (46-47), and engaged the residents of Lasell Village into the life of the College (49).

Successfully changing the institution's name from Lasell Junior College to Lasell: A Two-Year College for Women (34), then moving to become a four-year institution (34, 49-51) and soon thereafter to be co-educational (39-42, 43-44) required unusual political skills and acumen to overcome the reluctance of the Board as well as students and alumnae. By his own admission, he was less skillful politically in dealing with the College's neighbors (47) ("I'm a red flag to them.") but adroitly developed the arena in which to successfully compete with other colleges (50-51).

DeWitt skillfully employed the symbolic historical role of reputation of the College (32-33) to remind people of the role it once played, enhanced that symbol by investing in technology and facilities (38), demonstrated and restored the faith people, including Board members, had in the College through successful fundraising (38-39) and in going co-ed (39-42). Without question, as attested by his own comments, the conceptualization, development, and eventual opening of Lasell Village (36, 42-43, 47, 48-49) had great symbolic meaning ("Everyone saw this as the linchpin of Lasell's recovery...It gave everyone hope.").

Dr. Peggy A. Stock and Colby-Sawyer College

One of Stock's first acts was structurally reframing the campus ("...it was awful.") through improving its appearance by painting buildings and upgrading the grounds, building athletic and recreation centers, and refurbishing residence halls (56, 59-61). Going co-ed (57-59, 64) was a major structural change as was the elimination of some academic programs (61-62). She also made significant structural changes in the Board of Trustees (58, 61, 63-64).

Improving the campus' appearance improved morale (56). She adroitly handled alcoholics and sexual harassers on the faculty (57) and creatively retooled and reoriented a member of the faculty into a new teaching capacity (65). Although she was successful in identifying a strong supportive administrator (57,61), the personal toll and stress of the position were compelling (62, 65-66).

Going coed was against the grain of students, alumnae, and many Board members; however, Stock's political skills and acumen in engaging the support of an alumna Board member won the day (57-60, 64). Given the nature of faculty politics, she was nonetheless successful politically in eliminating academic programs (61-62). At the time of appointment, she boldly confronted the Board saying, "I'm going to push and nudge you and be a pain in the neck." (56)

Improving the appearance of the campus (56, 59-61) brought the symbolism of a revitalized and reinvigorated institution as did her successes in fundraising (64) ("...I raised $35 million for that small place.").

Dr. Jerry C. Lee and National University

Lee undertook a number of structural changes at the outset, including closing some poor performing centers (72) ("A School of Engineering without one lab"), developing faculty governance and policies and procedures (72, 73), overturning an unwieldy and overloaded senior administrative infrastructure (72-73) ("We had fourteen vice presidents for a university of seven thousand people"), reconstituting the Board (73-74), instituting cost control by focusing more on expenses than revenue (75-76), and developing a reliable accounting system (76) ("...the accounting system...[was] a very foreign form of bookkeeping").

His concern for people was demonstrated by initially denying salaries for himself and some senior administrators in order to pay faculty and staff (70), working with creditors (71-72) ("It wasn't a contract, it was just my word"), and supporting victims of domestic violence to get an education (74-75).

One of Lee's first steps demonstrated his political sensitivity and skill in deciding to present his case to the regional accrediting association (69) ("Thank goodness they said, 'We believe you'") and closing the Law School by engaging practitioners and judges as evaluators of the program (76).

Symbolically, he urged everyone to remember the institution's mission (70) saying, "...if we hang together, work together, and believe in the cause, many things can be overcome." This, along with other strategies, was instrumental in building a sense of community and a sense of pride (72, 74).

Dr. Robert E. Knott and Tusculum College

Instances of structurally reframing the College were renovating and reclaiming buildings (81, 85-86) ("...physically, the campus looked tired"), reconstituting the Board with more alumni (81-82) and with specific expectations (90), reconstructing the curriculum (82-83) ("...driven...around the mission statement"), bringing three former associates to his top team at the outset of his tenure (84), and reconstituting the athletic program (88-89).

The success of the first capital campaign "...brought a new sense of confidence to the Board" (83). This, coupled with empowering the faculty on curricular change (84-85, 87-88) and the positive impact that had on students (85), are exemplary of his concern for human resources, which was further demonstrated by his concern about faculty burn out (85) and fragility (88) and the need for a different president who could focus on fundraising (86).

Knott's political acumen was amply demonstrated by persuading the local banks to provide an initial loan of $2 million (81) followed by the issuance of bonds (83-84, 85-86, 89-90) and the dare of embarking on an initial capital campaign against all the professional advice (81).

Adopting a new mission statement that reclaimed the old traditions of the civic republican and Judeo-Christian heritage of education (82-83) was highly symbolic as was the initiation of the "side-porch" discussions of writings by one of the founders of the College, Cicero, and others (87-88). Preserving the then nearly two hundred year-old residential college against "...a fairly conscious move among officers of the Board" (88) was decidedly symbolic. Transforming and modernizing the physical plant was greeted enthusiastically by visiting alumni (87) as a symbol of renewed vitality.

Dr. Garry D. Hays and United States International University

Hays employed a number of strategies in structurally reframing the University: trimming the top heavy administration (96, 97-98) ("I inherited nine vice presidents and eight deans for a little place like this"); bringing in consultants in each academic area, closing weak programs, and redesigning others (97); hiring a new senior management group (98); addressing facilities and technology needs (98) ("Technology was non-existent - even the library had no technology"); closing the London campus after a protracted period of time and with considerable legal expense (100-101); creatively restructuring the $28 million debt through a purchase of the USIU campus by a private, non-profit group (102-104); and reconstituting the athletic · program to be financially successful (106-107).

164

He adroitly began to address faculty morale by starting the remodeling of faculty offices in the first year (98) and deferring until several years later refurbishing the fire-damaged administration building (99-100). He demonstrated confidence in the faculty and worked at re-engaging them in institutional affairs (98-99) through developing a faculty senate and shared governance (99) ("We had good faculty who suffered all those years [under the dictatorial founding president]") He also worked at re-engaging the staff, reminding them of the ripple effect of their independent actions and a "cover your ass mentality" (100).

His political skills were evident in repairing the relationship with the regional accrediting body by being "open and candid" unlike the founding president who, among other devious actions, never disclosed the existence of the foreign campuses (96-97) and "in joining every possible city group I could" (101).

One of Hays' most significant challenges was highly symbolic, namely changing the "rock bottom image" of the University by becoming heavily engaged in the community, working with the local newspapers, and making the new athletic facility more widely available (104-107).

Dr. Alan E. Guskin and Antioch University

Guskin employed a number of structural strategies in turning Antioch around: instituting strong budget controls in collecting full tuition instead of only 85 to 90 percent (114) and not sanctioning overrunning budgets (114); closing the Law School because it was losing money and lacked quality faculty and students (115-116) as well as closing two campuses that were marginal in quality and combining two other campuses (116-117); getting the Board to pass a resolution on having balanced budgets and then implementing it, because the chief financial officer said it couldn't be done, by approving all expenditures, even for $2.35, and firing a dean for overrunning his budget (116); reconstituting the Board and providing leadership in defining its roles and responsibilities (*e.g.,*"Give, Get, or Go") instead of micromanaging (118-120) ("They were going around the country with the chief financial officer developing the budgets of the various campuses.")

Encountering serious problems with staff not knowing what to do and/or not doing their jobs (*e.g.,* answering mail), especially in admissions, he worked to get them focused on their responsibilities (117-118). Guskin was very sensitive to the nature of Antioch students as mavericks, as were some of the faculty, and accommodated accordingly (118, 121). He acknowledged that in being a president, one is dealing with the minds of people and creating an institution in which people can grow and create (123).

Getting the Chair of the Board instead of himself to politic the Board about closing the Law School was a skillful political move (115-116). Likewise his adroit perception of how to be a strong leader in an inherently collaborative institution enabled him to be autocratic and authoritative at the beginning lest the institution die ("...the place was essentially bankrupt and twelve months away from closing") but to be his usual collaborative self when conditions improved (122).

There was great symbolism in closing the Law School instead of the College (115-116) ("There is no Antioch without the College") and then funding the College up front with the rest of the University supporting it (116-117). Also symbolic was developing a mantra of quality throughout the entire institution (117). Firing the dean who overran his budget was a case of theater in which an actor was playing his role poorly. Guskin had a passion and commitment to the values of Antioch and recognized that the symbolic role of an effective president is what he called the "priestly function"(123-124).

Dr. Stephen C. Morgan and the University of La Verne

Morgan immediately undertook a strategic structural step in appointing an Options Committee that was charged with finding ways to reduce expenditures and/or increase revenue in order to develop realistic budgets (130). Other structural strategies were: developing a strategic plan (131-132); having on-campus, full-time faculty involved in the off-campus, adult programs to provide quality assurance (134-135); balancing undergraduate and adult off-campus enrollments to render financial stability (135-136); developing a new faculty governance system (136-137); beginning to position the School of Law for American Bar Association accreditation (138-139); and forming a School of Education to bring all of the Education programs, the greatest academic strength of the University, under one umbrella (139).

Concern for people and the atmosphere in which they work and study led him to quickly "prime the pump" to begin campus beautification (130-131) ("We weren't attractive to students or employees"). He empowered faculty, students, and trustees by having them involved in strategic planning (131-132) and improved faculty morale through "good fortune and good luck...[and] hard work and strategy" (136), including closing the communication gap with faculty (136-137). He kept the Board well informed and spent time presupposing their questions on new proposals (136). Perhaps the most strategic human resource strategy was the identification of the student clientele best served by the University (132, 137, 140-141).

Morgan's political acumen was demonstrated early by persuading the University's banks to provide a larger line of credit and to allow a longer term for pay-back (129-130). He also developed good working relationships with the City of La Verne (138).

Recruiting his wife as an unpaid employee to beautify the campus was a symbolic maneuver to improve morale (130-131). ("The physical plant was a disaster"). Likewise were his efforts to correct the "negative public image of the University" (132-133) and successfully fundraise from individuals and foundations (134, 137-138). Finally, he had "...a real missionary zeal for what places like La Verne do with the students we serve" (140-141).

Neil J. Hoffman and Otis College of Art and Design

The first structural undertaking Hoffman made was to initiate long-range planning in his first month because there was a lack of vision and poor institutional climate (146). Further, he created an enrollment management approach in which everyone was involved and through which admissions standards were raised to meet institutional goals (147-148, 151). During the planning process, a faculty governance system was developed (150-151). In addition to initiating long-range planning, the move of the campus from its original location in a crime-ridden neighborhood in downtown Los Angeles to the safety of the west side (151) were critical structural actions that were crucial to salvaging the institution.

Throughout his interview, there are many examples of his deep and abiding concern for people as evidenced by: benefitting from a core of very good, loyal faculty and trustees (146); engaging everyone in a planning process that "...brought the community together"(147); having his performance evaluated by an outside consultant (147); engaging faculty in the enrollment management approach that resulted in a shared relationship with the lives of students (147); providing constructive performance evaluations of employees (153-154); and empowering heads of departments to do creative thinking ("...like Mark Twain, I was empowering them to paint the fence") (148-149). He got the Board to be actively involved in fund-raising (150) and helped other presidents understand the fundamentals of raising funds (152-153).

Symbolically, the planning process lead to a clear vision and set of eight goals for the College's future that were achieved (151). Likewise, the success in raising, at the time of the interview, $14 toward a $16 million campaign when previous fundraising was minuscule implied that the new vision was in fact being recognized beyond the campus (149-150).

Summary and Conclusion

As evidenced by the foregoing analyses, which are summarized in Table 1 (p. 170 *et. seq.*), these nine president were successful salvagers of institutions in various stages of *in extremis* by not looking for a magical silver bullet but rather by using a variety of reframing strategies and actions. Like a skilled carpenter who uses a variety of tools to accomplish a task, each of these presidents employed multiple tools - structural, human resources, political, symbolic - some unique to the peculiarities of the institution they served (*e.g.*, going co-ed at Colby Sawyer and Lasell University, refinancing through a private, non-profit corporation at United States International University) and some common to some or most of the institutions (*e.g.*, restructuring and training the Board, persuading local banks to extend lines of credit, building a faculty governance system).

As structural reframers, these salvaging presidents did their homework, finding out the root causes of the institution's difficulty (*e.g.,* Lee's finding overstaffing and lack of solid budget information at National University), thinking through the relationship of structure, strategy, and environment (*e.g.,* Knott's recognition of a weak Board with few alumni at Tusculum College), focusing on implementation (*e.g.,* Stock going co-ed at Colby Sawyer College and deWitt doing so at Lasell University), and evaluating and adapting as conditions changed (*e.g.,* Antioch's Guskin's being authoritarian at the beginning and then collaborative later).

As human resource reframers, these salvaging presidents demonstrated their belief in people and communicated it (e.g., Hays' painting faculty offices before repairing the fire-damaged administration building at United States International University), being visible and accessible (e.g., Knott's initiating the "side porch" discussions with faculty at Tusculum College), and empowering others (*e.g.,* Hoffman's challenging senior managers to develop creative ideas to improve admissions and retention at Otis College of Art and Design).

As political reformers, these presidents clarified what they wanted and what they could get (*e.g.,* Morgan's persuading the banks to provide a larger line of credit and longer payback at the University of La Verne), assessing the distribution of power and interests (*e.g.,* Averill's figuring out how to circumvent entrenched faculty leadership at Palo Verde College), building linkages to key stakeholders (*e.g.,* Stock's working with her alumna Board chair to win over alumnae on going co-ed), persuading, negotiating and even using coercion (*e.g.,* deWitt's admonition to his Board about the need to go co-ed and getting the Chair of the Board to persuade and negotiate with other members of the Board at Lasell College).

As symbolic reformers, these presidents used symbols to capture attention (*e.g.,* Averill's getting faculty and recalcitrant Board members to focus on the Future Research project at Palo Verde College), inspire (*e.g.,* Lee's urging everyone to remember the institution's mission at National University), discover and communicate a vision (*e.g.,* DeWitt's creation of Lasell Village), and tell stories (*e.g.,* Knott's reclaiming of the old traditions of the civic republican and Christian heritage of education at Tusculum College).

Given the range and variety of reframing strategies, it is evident that these salvaging presidents were successful because they were not narrow or mechanical thinkers and managers but instead were creative and even daring leaders. These presidents were, in Bolman and Deal's (1977) terms "...able to develop unique alternatives and novel ideas about what the organization needs. They are better attuned to people and events around them...The result is managerial freedom - and more productive human organizations" (p. 17).

Further, as was evident throughout the case studies and their analyses, these successful salvaging presidents were able, as Bolman and Deal note, to see the same organization simultaneously as machine, family, jungle, and theater. That required a capacity to think in different ways at the same time about the same thing.

Table 1. Summary of Reframing Actions Taken by the Nine Presidents

	Structural Frame	Human Resources Frame	Political Frame	Symbolic Frame
Donald Averill and Palo Alto College	Board development Adherence to law Relations with CSU-Chico and CSU-San Bernardino Programs for prison employees and farming community	Resolution of litigation issues Attention to due process Non-termination of employees and Board members Board training Addressing faculty concerns	Engendering community support Re-instituting non-credit courses Economic diversity development with City of Blythe Re-establishing ties to Community College Chancellor's Office Speeding up faculty contract negotiations Use of "canal diplomacy"	Future Research project involving faculty and Board members Developing program review model
Thomas deWitt and Lasell College	Staff training in operations management Conversion to four-year college and then to co-ed Building a business	"Getting everybody on board" Empowering the Board Re-hiring and empowering faculty Building a strong administrative team	Name change to Lasell: A Two-Year College for Women. then to four-year and later to co-ed Appointing an ombuds-person to deal with	Reminding people of the role Lasell once played Investing in technology and facilities Successful fundraising restoring faith in the

	climate Retrofitting business center to day-care Monthly information to the Board Investing in technology and facilities Designing Lasell Village	New procedures for evaluating the president Engaging Lasell Village residents in the life of the College	neighbors Successfully competing with other colleges	College Improving campus appearance Successful fundraising
Peggy Stock and Colby-Sawyer College	Improving appearance of the campus Building athletic and recreation center Refurbishing residence halls Going co-ed Elimination of some academic programs Changes in Board membership	Improving campus appearance improved morale Decisions regarding alcoholic and sexual harassers Retooling a faculty member Identifying a strong, supportive administrator	Going co-ed Eliminating some academic programs	
Jerry Lee and National University	Closing poorly performing centers Developing governance Slimming senior administrative	Initially denying salaries for self and senior administrators in order to pay faculty and staff	Meeting with regional accrediting association to win support Closing Law School	Reminding everyone of the Mission to build a sense of community and pride

	infrastructure Reconstituting the Board Instituting cost control Developing a reliable accounting system	Supporting victims of domestic violence		
Robert Knott and Tusculum College	Renovating and reclaiming buildings Reconstituting the Board with more alumni Reconstructing the curriculum around the Mission Employing three former associates Reconstituting the athletic program	Successful capital campaign brought confidence to the Board Empowering the faculty on curricular change Concern about faculty burn-out and fragility Recognizing need for a new president with fundraising abilities	Persuading local banks to provide an initial loan Issuance of bonds Embarking on an initial capital campaign	Adopting new Mission Statement that reclaimed the old traditions "Side-Porch" discussions Preserving the residential College Transforming and modernizing the physical plant
Garry Hays and United States International University	Trimming a top-heavy administration Remodeling faculty offices Hiring consultants in each academic area Closing weak programs	Remodeling faculty offices Developing a faculty senate and shared governance Re-engaging staff, reminding them of the	Repairing relationships with the regional accrediting agency about the existence of foreign campuses	Changing the image of the University by working with local media, and making the athletic facility available to the public

	and redesigning others Addressing facilities and technology needs Closing the London campus Restructuring the $28 million debt and Chapter 11 Reconstituting the athletic program	of the "ripple effect" of their independent actions		Closing the Law School instead of Antioch College Funding the College with support from other units Developing a mantra of quality throughout the institution Firing a dean who overran his budget Recognizing the "priestly function" of an effective president
Alan Guskin and Antioch University	Instituting strong budget controls Closing the Law School and two marginal campuses and combining two others Getting the Board to pass a resolution on balanced budgets Reconstituting the Board and defining its responsibilities	Getting staff focused on their responsibilities Accommodating to the maverick nature of Antioch students and faculty Acknowledging that a president deals with the minds of people and creating an institution in which people can grow and create	Getting the Board Chair to politic members to close the Law School Being autocratic at the outset and collaborative later when conditions improved	

Stephen Morgan and the University of La Verne	Appointing an Options Committee on expenditures and revenue; Developing a strategic plan; Involving on-campus faculty in off-campus programs; Balancing undergraduate and off-campus program enrollments; Developing a new faculty governance system; Positioning the Law School for ABA accreditation; Consolidating all Education programs in a School of Education	Beginning campus beautification; Empowering faculty, students, and trustees by involving them in strategic planning; Improving faculty morale by closing the communication gap; Keeping the Board well informed and anticipating their questions on new proposals; Identifying the student clientele best served by the University	Persuading banks to provide a larger line of credit; Developing relationships with the City of La Verne	Beautification of the campus to improve morale; Correcting the negative public image of the University; Successful fundraising; Having a missionary zeal for the University
Neil Hoffman and Otis College of Art and Design	Initiating long-range planning; Creating an enrollment	Working with very good and loyal faculty and trustees		Planning process that led to clear vision and setting eight goals

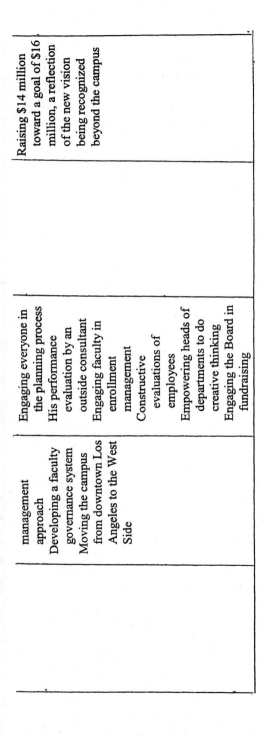

		Raising $14 million toward a goal of $16 million, a reflection of the new vision being recognized beyond the campus
management approach Developing a faculty governance system Moving the campus from downtown Los Angeles to the West Side	Engaging everyone in the planning process His performance evaluation by an outside consultant Engaging faculty in enrollment management Constructive evaluations of employees Empowering heads of departments to do creative thinking Engaging the Board in fundraising	

Part Four: Overview and Analysis of the Survey Results

To recapitulate the research protocol briefly, forty-nine presidents who had salvaged their institutions, most of whom were identified with the confidential assistance of four of the six regional accrediting associations, were sent a survey instrument. Thirty-six completed the survey, which, with their responses, is found in the Appendix A. This section provides an overview and analysis of the survey responses.

The survey was designed to draw out information about: (1) the situation at the institution when the new president arrived; (2) the reasons the president believes were important in being appointed; (3) the short-term actions and long-term strategies for the turnaround; (4) the turnaround; and (5) advice for other presidents.

The Situation(s) Encountered

Thirty-one of the thirty-six presidents who participated in the survey identified lack of institutional and program planning as the major institutional issue they encountered. Essentially, their institutions didn't know where they were going nor were they searching for where to go. This issue was followed closely by: their institution's very small endowment, often because it had been dipped into to meet current operations; financial exigency due to plunging enrollments and overspent budgets; negative public image of the institution because of poor leadership and financial difficulties; and inadequate fundraising because of a lack of experience and/or will. In virtually all of the cases, the institution's finances and its public image were in disrepair.

Even though these presidents did reasonable due diligence and thought they had a good handle on the problems before arriving on campus, without exception things looked worse to most of them after being on the job a few months. The problems were deeper and broader than they thought. As Donald Averill, of Palo

Verde College, noted, "Sometimes Boards don't tell you everything." On the other hand, sometimes Boards don't tell because they were not sufficiently engaged in their work to know what the financial situation was. Also, sometimes senior officers don't tell the Board the severity of problems lest they jeopardize their jobs. Further, van der Werf (2002) cited a Standard and Poor report, "Weak Equity Market Hurt U. S. Education Endowments," that suggests the accounting procedures used by colleges are inconsistent, potentially hiding financial problems.

At the time of appointment, about a third of the presidents were fully aware of the issues such that there were no surprises within the first month of two, but nearly half of these presidents had come from inside the institution. To varying degrees, other presidents discovered or encountered previously unknown matters that added further difficulty to the salvaging operation. For example, Paul LeBlanc noted, "The worst was discovering how unrealistic was the budget I inherited." Laurence Conner found an accelerating negative impact on all constituencies by being placed on probation by the North Central Association of Colleges and Schools Colleges, a rift among Trustees, and distrust by some Trustees of the administration because of a clandestine effort that had been attempted to separate from affiliate organizations. Francis Hazard, of Urbana University, noted that a "Majority of trustees were acting like absentee landlords." At the University of West Los Angeles, Edward Kormondy noted "Five of eight senior positions, including that of the President, were in acting status owing to resignations and terminations over a six-month period."

Alan Guskin knew that Antioch University's facilities "...were terrible," administrative systems were in disrepair, and morale was very low but later learned that the institution was eight to twelve months from closing, the Board was exhausted, key administrative people didn't really know what they were doing and didn't feel they could solve the problems. Richard Wylie, of Endicott College, noted that the "Board was entertaining proposals for sale, banks refused to lend money, and loss of D&O insurance." Golden Gate University's Thomas Stauffer said that he knew most of the issues but more by instinct because many in the old regime did not appreciate the seriousness of the situation; however, he later found that finances, technology, policy, and other matters were worse than anybody knew.

At National University, Jerry Lee indicated that although most of the conditions were known to him, he was unaware of their depth and severity and later learned of decreasing enrollments and that not only was the Board improperly constituted, he lacked its support. At Urbana University, Francis Hazard subsequently found a weak admissions and development staff, poor to non-existent alumni relations, poor public image, lack of bank and vendor credit, and misplaced enrollment dependent on prison contracts with the state that proved to be unreliable. Tusculum College's Robert Knott was aware beforehand of low morale, a weak Board, and low enrollment and graduation rates but subsequently learned of the severity of financial problems and the considerable level of deferred maintenance. Paul Le Blanc found "A good but aging Board suffering from 'Board Fatigue.'"

Characteristics of Salvaging Presidents

The search committees and boards who selected these "salvaging presidents" were apparently aware of some but seemingly not all of these major institutional issues, because they hired presidents who had the experience to address them. Thirty-one of the thirty-six presidents believed that they were selected for the depth and breadth of their senior administrative experience, including several with experience with other turnaround situations. Other reasons for their selection that were mentioned often were experience in planning, financial management, public relations, and fundraising. Most of the presidents, therefore, believe that they were chosen for reasons that matched their institution's needs. But, Chatt Wright, of Hawai'i Pacific University, noted, "Problems so severe, no one would want the position," and Stephen Morgan, of the University of La Verne, indicated, "I was the lesser of two or three evils."

With regard to the specifics of pertinent experience, all but two of the respondents had served at various levels of and for differing numbers of years in academic administration, most in vice presidential (fifteen) or previous presidential (seven) positions, and with only a few exceptions in more than one institution. For example, Michael Bassis, of Olivet College, had five years of turnaround experience as Executive Vice President of another institution. A number had worked in the for-profit private sector (*e.g.*, General Motors and Commercial Credit Corporation - Jerry Lee, of National University); not for-profit private sector (*e.g.,* American Council on Education - Thomas Stauffer, of Golden Gate University); accrediting commissions (*e.g.,* Commission on Colleges of the Southern Association of Schools and Colleges and the United Board for College Development - Haywood Strickland, of Texas University); governmental agency (*e.g.,* senior administrator in Federal government and the military (Chief of Staff at the rank of Major General in the Air National Guard) - Francis Hazard, of Urbana University).

Of the two with no previous academic administrative experience, Kent Keith had been an attorney, head of a state agency, and a businessman (high tech park developer); further, he was a Protestant, and Chaminade University of Honolulu was and is Catholic. Also lacking previous academic administrative experience was Daniel Ritchie, of the University of Denver, who had extensive experience in corporate management and had also served as Vice Chair of the University's Board of Trustees and chair of its Development Committee.

Short-Term Actions and Long-Term Strategies

Thirty-five of the thirty-six presidents in the survey began immediately to meet with faculty, and most met also with their Board and staff. Eighteen met with accrediting bodies, and fifteen with students and community leaders. The theme of their short-term actions was to meet, listen, ask questions, and share information - to learn the culture. In the Bolman and Deal (1997) theoretical model, these presidents were structural leaders doing their homework to determine what the problems were and the nature of the institution's environment.

The meetings that characterized the short-term actions of the presidents laid the foundation for the strategy mentioned by thirty-two presidents as their long-term strategy: long-range/strategic planning, a structural reframing of their respective institution. Their institutions didn't know where they were going, so it was necessary to chart a course by creating a long-term plan. At Chaminade University of Honolulu, Kent Keith held workshops "...with faculty, staff, and Regents to develop a three year plan to respond to [the] WASC [Western Association of Schools and Colleges] accreditation report." Mentioned nearly as often were training the Board in regard to its role, strategic planning, instituting new student recruitment programs, and improving relationships between the administration and faculty as well as between the institution and the community.

While long-range or strategic planning was mentioned most often by the presidents as their long-term strategy, it did not rank high as their *most effective* strategy in turning things around. The most effective strategy was general organizational development. As Laurence Conner stated, "I began the first downsizing phase, and as conditions worsened, a more carefully planned but quickly executed 'right sizing' phase II began with every aspect of the University modified at some level."

Next in importance to organizational development in the turnaround were fiscal planning, enrollment management, public relations, and strengthening and/or reconstituting the board. Only ten presidents mentioned strategic planning as their most effective strategy.

The Turnaround

Since general organizational development was the presidents' most effective strategy in the turnaround, it is not surprising that thirty-three of the presidents identified their leadership skills. Nearly as many mentioned their communication and organizational management skills as well as their personality attributes, experience, and/or background as playing most heavily in achieving the turnaround. For Paul LeBlanc, it was a case of "Energy, entrepreneurial spirit, building an excellent management team, reenergizing faculty." Similarly, for Michael Bassis, of Olivet College, it was "Persistence, courage, focus, resolve." Twenty-seven also mentioned their skills in strategic planning, interpersonal relations, and public relations as important in their salvaging efforts.

Seventeen of the respondents indicated that the turnaround took two to five years, nine indicated one to two years, eight were still in process after two months or three to four years, two indicated more than five years, and none less than one year. Alan Guskin indicated it took less than a year to stop the bleeding at Antioch but two to four years to refocus the institution. At United States International University, Garry Hays noted that it took less than a year to review the mission and make personnel changes, one to two years to develop financial and strategic plans, two to five years for changes in academic and student life programs, and that it was still on-going six years after starting the turnaround. Although Stephen Morgan indicated it took two to five years at the University of La Verne, he noted it was still on-going after thirteen years!

In short, the presidents found institutions that didn't know where they were going. They immediately held meetings with faculty, board members, and other constituents, and they developed long-term strategies and plans to give their institutions a new sense of direction. However, developing long-term strategies and implementing them are not the same thing. Implementing the strategies required organizational development--the strategy that most presidents mentioned as the most effective strategy in accomplishing the turnaround. The skills that helped the presidents bring about that organizational development were leadership, communication, and organizational management, followed by strategic planning, interpersonal, and public relations skills.

Advice for Presidents

Unlike the preceding sections, we have built on the advice offered to prospective salvaging presidents from the survey by expanding on some of the key responses based on our own experience, and that of others, including search firm personnel in our acquaintance.

In response to the kind of advice to be proffered to presidents selected to salvage an institution, none advised not to do it. However, having made the decision to accept the presidency, making sure one has Board support was mentioned most frequently. It most certainly is a *sine qua non* of any successful presidency that Board support is critical. Having that support demonstrable from the outset is even more critical in an institution that must be turned around. In announcing the presidential appointment, the Chair and/or Executive Committee, should clearly articulate the problems the institution faces, which may or may not be widely understood by the collegiate community, and the specific experience and skills the new president has in being able to address them. Even though the president's experience would have been evident to those involved in the search, it is quite likely not to be widely known, especially in larger institutions. This evidence of support at the outset but especially in the turnaround, as attested by our salvaging presidents, was of singular importance.

Nearly as many of the presidents indicated the importance of accepting the position with "your eyes wide open" and making sure there was access to all critical information. For a number of the salvaging presidents, it would appear that although their eyes might have been wide open, all of the critical information was either held back or was unknown even to those who should have known, such as Board members. In the latter instance, senior administrative officials may have knowingly withheld such information for fear of loss of their position or may not have had the competence to identify such information. Thus, it behooves a presidential candidate, salvaging or not, to have access to: 1) the most recent regional accrediting agency report as well as those of any specialized accrediting bodies, and if such reports cite previous issues of concern, those reports should be examined; 2) the most recent financial audit along with those of the previous two or three years; 3) monthly budget reports from beginning of the current fiscal year; 4) enrollment history; 5) scholarship awards (*i.e.*, discount rate); and 6) fundraising effectiveness *(e.g.,* trustee and alumni giving, most recent capital campaign), amongst other pertinent information.

Given these suggestions, it was of surprise to us to note that several very experienced individuals had not done their homework before assuming the presidency of prestigious universities. In their study of eight research university presidents, Brodie and Banner (2005) noted that seven of the presidents described themselves as unprepared in some crucial area or areas of institutional knowledge. For example, Vartan Gregorian with experience as a dean at the University of Pennsylvania before heading the New York Public Library, noted about assuming the role of president at Brown University in 1988 that there were certain things that were not volunteered and that he did not ask about. "I had not done an exhaustive study; I had not done a great deal of homework" (p.310). Similarly, Benno Schmidt, whose career included being Dean of Columbia University Law School, admitted that only after accepting the presidency of Yale University in 1986 did he realize the seriousness of its financial strains and maintenance problems.

As noted several times above, the candidate should endeavor to learn the culture of the institution as the first step in conceptualizing structural reframing strategies. As is generally acknowledged, unless leaders understand the culture, they will not be able to meet the challenges. Bensimon (1990) indicated that presidents had to be "cultural knowers," understanding the lived experience of the campus. As noted in the earlier section on short-and long-term strategies, thirty-five of the thirty-six presidents immediately began meeting with a variety of groups to listen, ask questions, and share information. Depending on the institution, this led to awareness of both the internal and external forces (*e.g.*, demographic, social, economic, political) affecting the institution. This sensitization to the cultural climate enabled these salvaging presidents to recognize how things had been done, which may have been factors leading to the source of the problems at hand, and then moving strategically in reframing the institutions by changing behaviors, policies, and processes.

Having skills in organizational development is a key attribute in a salvaging president and was identified as the most effective turnaround strategy. It is indeed difficult to lead a process of change without having the Board behind you and all the facts in front of you. However, if one cannot effect an organizational structure that can address the issues, a turnaround will not occur. This involves, as Bolman and Deal (1997) noted being able to look at problems from more than one perspective. Bensimon and Neumann (1993) suggested bringing together diverse minds, with the teamwork generating creative problem solving. At Tusculum College, Bob Knott brought along three people (a chief admissions officer, a chief development officer, and an associate development officer) with whom he had worked for varying periods of time, "...so we were able to hit the ground running just within days of getting here." Richard Cox noted, "Make sure you have a team that is committed to the same plan and committed to the long haul." Neil Hoffman's approach at one point in his career was to assemble his department heads every Monday where each one had to bring in two creative ideas on improving services to students, being more efficient, and improving conversion and retention rates. This is not only an excellent strategy for empowerment, it developed a sense of a team - diverse people creating new stratagems. As Garry Hays, of United States International University, noted, "Bring in, or find within the institution, good people to help and whom you can trust."

There is both a upside and downside to effecting a rapid change in the senior administrative team. In their study of eight research university presidents, Brodie and Banner (2005) noted that of the five presidents who spoke to the issue, three relied on continuity of the administrative team that was in place. For example, Harold Shapiro, who was President of the University of Michigan (1980-1987) and Princeton University (1988-2001) viewed it as a mistake to come into office and "...sweep clean unless there's some kind of crisis" (p. 171). By contrast, Donald Kennedy, who was President of Stanford University (1980-1992), felt if one didn't move fast to build one's own team, "...your decisions would appear to be whimsical" (p. 22).

Finally, as the respondents in our survey pointed out, a turnaround requires patience and energy on the part of individuals who can subsume their ego, be committed to a cause, enjoy a challenge, and, importantly, do it as a labor of love.

A Final Question

As noted above, none of the thirty-six respondents would advise other presidents to *not* lead a turnaround. During the in-depth interviews, the nine presidents were asked: "Would you do it again?" Even though the following responses of three of them were provided earlier, in our judgement they represent the best final advice to those who are considering a salvaging assignment.

Garry Hays, of United States International University, said:

> Yes, I would. This is the eighth year and it doesn't seem like it, frankly. Obviously, as you know, there are times when it can get frustrating, and you say are we ever going to get this done or that done. But, yes, I'd do it in a minute. It has been an extremely rewarding experience. I thought if we could pull it off in a situation like this, to really have an impact and to see the results would be great - and it has been.

Alan Guskin, of Antioch University, said:

> Yes, I would. It sounds crazy but I cannot imagine being a leader of any other institution than Antioch at that point of time that would have given me more meaning. In terms of a sense of purpose, there is nothing that will ever match that. If you create a new institution, maybe you can have the kind of experience I had, but, true or not, I feel I was literally President at a critical moment in the life of a great institution and what I did really made a difference. That doesn't mean nobody

else could have done it. But I was the one who did it, and so that gives me an enormous, extraordinary sense of meaning in life. It is something that gives me a sense of peace. It is very special... The Gods do exact a price for giving you the privilege of leading others ... I used to tell myself that what I was doing was not just for the people here today but for the future, the president's role is for the future. I loved it, it was a kick.

Robert Knott, of Tusculum College, was not so sure:

...(I)n my professional career I don't know that I have had anything any more rewarding professionally and personally than - seeing the College come back to its feet and regain stability and some momentum for the future - watching a Board go from being very tentative about what they could do and how they could lead to becoming quite confident, which was through the success of that first capital campaign - seeing a faculty go from being demoralized to having a real sense of commitment and spirit to what they believed and what they were doing with the curriculum and students - and watching a student body that didn't really have much pride in themselves and the College become one that came to really believe in themselves. That was all extremely rewarding to me, and I have not had another experience that was as rewarding as that. So would I do it again, Yes, knowing that it was out there as something to enjoy. Would I have taken it knowing all the financial strains and difficulties? Probably not.

Part Five: Lessons Learned

Lesson #1: Struggling Institutions Have a Lot in Common

As the analysis in Part Four indicates, all of the thirty-six institutions in the study demonstrated most if not all of Neil Hoffman's six characteristics of struggling institutions: lack of vision and mission, leadership, planning, and enrollment management; financial problems; and negative impact on institutional climate (pages 4 - 6). Thirty-one of the presidents indicated a lack of planning, which translates in large measure to a lack of vision and mission, the key starting point in a turn around.

Hoffman also opined that a struggling institution is one that has less than a million dollars in endowment. Although that indicator was not specifically asked of the presidents in the survey, twenty-nine of the thirty-six respondents noted that their institution had a very small endowment, and twenty-seven indicated there was financial exigency. The survey and the interviews made it clear that struggling institutions have a lot in common.

That financial exigency was identified as an important factor in these struggling institutions should not come as a surprise. Higher education in the United States has always faced fiscal stress. During the Colonial Period, Harvard as well as other colleges often survived through appropriation of public funds, and, in the nineteenth century, donations, developing endowments, discounting tuition (yes, even then), and low salaries to faculty and staff were often the means to survival (Rudolph, 1962).

The institutions in our survey showed varying degrees of what Sellars (2005), in his study of failed institutions, distinguished between controllable and uncontrollable factors, which concide to a large degree to the findings in our study as related in Parts Three and Four and Appendix A. Of controllable factors, he determined that the two strongest predictors of financial decline were the perception of academic quality and size of the student body; others were the percentage of budget allocated to scholarships and student aid and the percentage of annual revenue from gift and endowment income. Uncontrollable factors were regional demographics, economic influences, and the local community.

The institutions in our survey showed varying degrees of both controllable and uncontrollable factors. Among the controllable factors were declining or low enrollments (*e.g.* Antioch, Colby-Sawyer, and Lasell Colleges), academic programs of poor quality (*e.g.*, National University's engineering program without a lab), and low fundraising revenues (most of the institutions in our survey). Among the uncontrollable factors were regional demographics (*e.g.,* University of La Verne's dependence for enrollment on the region), economic influences (*e.g.,* United States International University being $28 million in debt as well as in Chapter 11), and the local community (*e.g.,* the negative perception of the University of La Verne because of its financial problems).

In their study of thirteen institutions in stress, Leslie and Fretwell (1996) noted that the sources of the fiscal stress were indeed complex. In some of the institutions, external changes in public policies regarding funding are among the uncontrollable factors cited by Sellers (2005), but also the lack of prudent planning and managing contributed to the crises in these institutions.

Lesson #2: It Takes Courage to Lead a Turnaround

Before accepting their positions, the presidents in our survey knew enough about the situations on their campuses to know that it would be tough. They had the courage to assume the responsibility for a turnaround. After arriving on campus, however, most of them found that the situation was even worse than they thought. However, they had the courage to stick it out.

In her first month, the president who was the tenth interviewee but who withdrew her interview on the advice of her Board chair learned there was a $1.5

million financial aid problem, a residence hall burned to the ground, the College did not have a line of credit and thus couldn't meet the September 15th payroll, and the College had a non-contributory retirement plan. Nonetheless, she persevered against these stacked odds and eventually turned the institution around.

Eleven days after he arrived at Palo Verde College, Don Averill received a letter from the accrediting commission putting his College on probation and giving him only six months to come up with an interim report to solve the problems. He was undaunted, tackling each of a number of problems head on.

Peggy Stock was immediately faced with a $625,000 deficit at Colby-Sawyer College and, with enrollments already at a nadir, there were only a paltry forty-four applicants for the fall term. This was coupled with virtually no endowment and a neglected campus that "...was a travesty, an embarrassment." Nonetheless, "I relentlessly did the job." But, "...no one but my husband saw the anguish I went through."

Thomas deWitt started work when Lasell College was at a thirty-year low in enrollment, with millions of dollars in deferred maintenance. There were forty-three buildings for 393 students; many of the buildings were empty. The budget was being balanced by selling property. DeWitt had the courage to champion a new future for the College by its becoming first a four-year institution and then going co-ed. It caused a falling out, beginning with the Executive Committee, "...which went ballistic." DeWitt didn't back down. He led the board and then a joint committee of trustees, faculty, and staff through his projections and analyses, as well as a look at other institutions that had gone co-ed. The initial opposition changed, the Committee recommended going co-ed, and the Board approved. The College had a new future.

When Jerry Lee assumed his position at National University, he found trouble with faculty governance and accreditation, lots of litigation, and an accounting system that couldn't track payables and receivables. The media were having a field day with the University, which had a poor reputation in the community. Lee had the courage to close schools and centers and cut the number of administrators. A bullet

came through his office window, and the police concluded it was not an accident—
it was shot on purpose. Lee's son, who was three years old, had to have an armed
guard protecting him on the way to kindergarten. Nonetheless, Lee stayed the course

Robert Knott arrived at Tusculum College expecting a balanced budget for
the year - having been told so by the Board - and discovered a $1.6 million deficit,
which the Board didn't know about. Even worse, there were no accountants in the
business office, and the chief financial officer was not an accountant, so the College
literally didn't know where it stood. Knott, his new chief financial officer, and key
trustees took action. They invited five bankers to meet with them to review a five-
year financial plan that was put together in two weeks. "We had no track record; we
had nothing but promises that we would try to make it work," Knott recalled. The
banks said yes. Undaunted, the courage of his conviction that the institution was
worth saving and restoring its significant heritage were essential in his being able to
salvage the College.

At United States International University, Garry Hays took on a campus that
had a $28 million debt and was in Chapter 11 bankruptcy. He had only a year to turn
around the debt situation to meet the terms of the court-approved three-year plan. The
University's major asset was its campus. In the end, help was found from a group of
non-profit organizations that created a new non-profit corporation to purchase the
USIU campus and become the Member of the USIU corporation, so it was more than
a landlord-tenant relationship. He never turned back

Alan Guskin left a palatial office at the University of Wisconsin-Parkside to
assume the presidency of Antioch University, where he found the Antioch College
campus with closed buildings and an enrollment of 400 students-- down from 1,200
in earlier years. The institution was essentially bankrupt, twelve months away from
closing. The University wasn't paying its bills or taxes and was borrowing to the hilt,
including borrowing from trustees. Only 85 to 90 percent of the tuition was being
collected, and people were overrunning their budgets. Guskin took control. He
immediately closed the law school and got the Board to pass a resolution that the

budget would be balanced, no matter what the pain. There was opposition from board members to closing the law school and opposition from staff to the balanced budget. But Guskin had the courage to put his job on the line. A trustee asked him, what would happen if the Board voted against closing the law school and balancing the budget? Guskin replied that the Board would have to look for a new president.

Stephen Morgan started at the University of La Verne when payroll was in doubt, and people rushed to the bank to deposit their paychecks. There were months when the University borrowed money from members of the Board of Trustees on a short-term basis, a hundred thousand here and a hundred thousand there, to meet payroll. There was almost no endowment, no cash, a short-term debt of $5 million, and a string of deficits. During his first week as President, he had a meeting with the University's bankers, who were trying to decide what to do. "I talked fast and furiously about plans and steps I planned to take immediately to turn us around; and I begged for a larger line of credit and more time," recalled Morgan. The banks decided to support the University, giving Morgan time to appoint the Options Committee that worked hard on reducing expenditures and increasing revenues. He never wavered from the will to turn the University around.

Neil Hoffman returned to Otis College of Art and Design to find a characteristically struggling institution with a lack of vision and mission and a lack of planning coupled with no leadership. Accreditation was critical, the endowment was only $300,000, and enrollment was flat. Hoffman started a long-range planning process, built faculty governance, and challenged campus supervisors to bring two creative ideas to their meeting each Monday - ideas about how to improve the quality of service to students, to be more efficient, to improve retention. He hired an outside consultant to interview fifty people about his own performance, as well as attending a retreat at which his strengths and weaknesses were analyzed. He worked toward empowering others. He believed strongly that the institution was worth saving. He led, he held firm - he won.

Even in a crisis, when the need for change is clear, individual attitudes and organizational cultures resist the new and unknown. It took courage for the presidents in our study to lead change, almost always with little time, few resources, and entrenched opposition. Further, these presidents exercised the two types of leadership that Birnbaum (1992) described: instrumental (*i.e.*, based on technical competence, experience, and judgment) and interpretive (*i.e.*, altering perception of institutional function). He regarded such presidents as "exemplary" because they,"...may have a major effect in renewing institutional values and improving organizational performance under certain circumstances" (p. 167).

Lesson #3: An Effective Board Is Crucial to a Turnaround

The singularly critical role of an effectively functioning governing board in the success of an institution is well acknowledged. Thanks to organizations like the Association of Governing Boards of Colleges and Universities (AGB), there is a considerable literature directing attention to the role and appropriate functioning of governing boards and their constituent members (*e.g.*, Ingram 1995). AGB has also been a leader in developing workshops and training sessions for boards as a whole and/or its committees. Gratifyingly, many boards that recognized they needed help have availed themselves of these services. Also, Zander (1993) has provided a comprehensively detailed set of recipes for board development and effective operation.

The importance of a properly functioning, constituted, and supportive board was a paramount concern for most of the presidents in our survey. Thirteen presidents noted lack of board support, ten checked micromanagement by their board, and ten noted improperly constituted boards as major institutional issues they encountered. Demonstrating the key role of their boards, thirty-three of the presidents immediately held meetings with their board. When it came to long-term strategies, thirty presidents initiated board training, and twenty undertook a reconstitution of the board.

The experience of several of the presidents who were interviewed is instructive. Thomas deWitt, of Lasell College, said that one thing he did very quickly when he became President was to send board members information every month, telling them what was happening on campus so that there were no surprises and educating the trustees about the role of higher education so they could better understand the issues facing colleges. DeWitt noted, "Boards really look to presidents to provide leadership and to mold the institution, they want no problems, they want to revel in the success and be proud of the institution, and that's why they give money." He also learned that getting very, very powerful and public figures is not an answer for small boards because they have no time for the board's business; they are just lending their name. Usually, he noted, they are not even the big givers and that the biggest givers tend to be alumni.

Jerry Lee, of National University, reported that he knew it wasn't a university board, "...nice, well-intentioned people, but not a university board." So his strategy was a recommendation to expand the board with three new slots, and those three new people were able to help him professionalize the board, raising it to another level. Some of the other board members began to feel uncomfortable and realized they were in a different league. So, by a gradual process, the composition of his board was changed.

Micromanagement by board members was a problem for many of the salvaging presidents. A prime example was the experience of Alan Guskin at Antioch University, making it difficult for him to lead and be held accountable. Antioch board members, including the chair of the finance committee, were going around the country with the chief financial officer of the University developing the budget with the various campuses. As he relayed it, these board members just loved the College and if there were a problem, they'd say, "We'll solve it," without realizing they should not be doing the president's work. Thus, the board had gotten into a state of confusion about what its role was, the result of poor leadership. Guskin realized that they had to be educated. So he told them about Kingman Brewster's three "G's" - "Give, Get, or Go," and he asked them to give money, get money, or leave the board, but not try to manage the institution. He reminded them that they had hired him to run the institution and to hold him accountable to do so.

Peggy Stock, of Colby-Sawyer College, with the help of three successive chairs, changed the composition of the Board significantly. These chairs were very supportive of major decisions, such as building a building, and one was of crucial support during the process of making the decision to go co-ed.

Robert Knott, of Tusculum College, reported that Bruce Alton, of the presidential search firm, Academic Search Consulting Service, left him and the Trustees a report in which he indicated seven or nine major points that the College needed to address. At or near the top was the need for reconstituting the board with people who had a more deeply felt sense of ownership of the College. Also the board had been recruited with no expectations, financial or otherwise. So he very deliberately set out that first year to create a Trusteeship Committee and through it to establish a list of expectations of Trustees. They were able to move rather quickly to get the board up to thirty. Also, whenever they found people who had the capacity to be major contributors, financial or otherwise, they were quick to invite them to come onto the Board. It was a very conscious effort to rebuild the board and to bring many more alumni on. On his arrival, out of twenty-one members, there were only four or five alumni; when they reached a membership of forty, some twenty were alumni, all of whom had a strong allegiance to the College.

Building boards and defining their roles so they could be effective was crucial to most of the presidents in our study. This generalization applies to many, if not most, institutions, struggling or not.

Lesson #4. Good Community Relations are Essential to a Turnaround

Patrick and Caruthers (1980) surveyed college and university presidents regarding their priorities among the potential planning and management improvements at their institutions. Their two highest priorities were communicating institutional strengths to potential students and their parents, followed by communicating institutional strengths to the general public. Public institutions also gave a high priority to communicating their institutional strengths to their primary publics - state legislatures and state budget officials.

The importance of communicating with the community is another lesson that can be drawn from the presidents in our study. Twenty-seven presidents listed their institution's negative public image as a major issue when they arrived on campus, nineteen mentioned public relations campaigns as long-term strategies, while eleven cited public relations as one of their most effective strategies.

In commenting on his experience at Palo Verde College, Donald Averill said that the key strategy he wanted to use was to move away from the internal constituencies, recognizing the institution needed the support of the community. He brought together representatives of the Unified School District, the prisons, the Chamber of Commerce, the City of Blythe staff, as well as students from the Unified School District and the College. He started meeting with all the constituent groups and finally got very active with them. He knew he had to get them back into the fold to move the College forward.

Robert Knott reached out to the community very soon after his arrival at Tusculum College. He recalled that they went immediately into a capital campaign against all the professional advice because they really hadn't gotten to know likely supporters at all. He was more than surprised and caught off guard by the willingness of people to respond, both in the local community and among the alumni. In retrospect, he believes this probably resulted from fear about losing the college, a fear that became a galvanizing force.

Garry Hays found that the "...challenge of external relations was a huge thing" at United States International University when he arrived. Fortunately, he also found that the community was open to somebody who would be candid with them and who had integrity. Hays went out into the community and gave what he called his "clearing of the deck speech." He noted that they had a PR firm do a survey of the movers and shakers in San Diego, including those with whom they had had an opportunity to talk and those with whom they hadn't. He found that if they had had an opportunity to be with people, talk to them, and tell them what was going on, the feedback about their impressions of USIU was quite different from those with whom they had not yet been in contact. Hays noted that this told them that their strategy was working - getting to people, telling them what is happening.

Lesson #5: The Strategic Solution to a Financial Crisis May Be Organizational Development

Resolving the financial crisis, typically consisting of a depleted endowment coupled with deficits extending over several years, was an immediate problem faced by most of the presidents in the survey. It is of interest to compare their responses to the results of a study by Hamlin and Hungerford (1988) of fifty-one colleges and universities that had experienced a severe financial crisis. From a list of thirty-nine factors in their study, the presidents were asked by Hamlin and Hungerford to identify those tools they had found to be most effective in overcoming the financial crisis. On a scale of 1 (no utility) to 4 (essential), the highest rankings were: expanded recruiting efforts (3.20), fundraising efforts of the president (3.18), gifts/grants from benefactors (3.00), public awareness efforts of the president (2.92), increasing tuition and fees (2.92), and increasing scholarship funding (2.90).

When the highest ranked factors were further ranked, expanding recruiting and fundraising efforts received the highest weighted average scores. Hamlin and Hungerford concluded: "The institutions that were successful in overcoming a financial crisis during the past decade did so using tools which [sic] were designed to *enhance revenue* rather than to decrease expenses" (p. 35).

In the Hamlin and Hungerford study, faculty/staff cutbacks and layoffs and administration cutbacks and layoffs were the third and fourth most essential tools, ranked after the expansion of recruiting and fundraising efforts. In our survey, half of the presidents did cut the budget as an immediate action, but cutbacks and layoffs did not rank high on the list of their long-term strategies, nor did most see budget cutting as one of the most effective strategies. Expenditure reduction, however, was high on the list of corrective actions for Jerry Lee, of National University who laid the pattern of the "growth by substitution and cost control," and Stephen Morgan, of the University of La Verne who immediately convened a group to look at expenditure reduction. In fact, when it came to long-term strategies of expenditure reduction, only two presidents mentioned closing a school or satellite campuses, and only one mentioned eliminating staff positions to hire more faculty.

When asked about the most effective strategies in turning around their situations, the presidents in our survey mentioned organizational development forty-two times, far more mentions than any other strategy. Fiscal planning, including cost reductions, was mentioned nineteen times. Revenue-enhancing measures were mentioned less often. Enrollment management activities were mentioned thirteen times, and development was mentioned nine times.

A possible reason for the differences between the Hamlin and Hungerford study and our survey may be that they selected institutions with financial crises, while the crises faced by the presidents in our survey included but were not limited to financial issues. The most effective response to the wide range of issues faced by the presidents in our study was organizational development.

One key element in organizational development for the presidents in our study was team-building at the senior management level. Bensimon and Neumann (1993) argued that since no one person can know everything, and since each person has different insights and abilities, "...the ideal leader will be someone who knows how to find and bring together diverse minds" (p.1) They noted that teamwork can generate creative problem solving among diversely oriented minds; it can facilitate cognitive complexity, such as using multiple frames or models in analyzing issues. Teams can provide peer support for the president and each other. Teams can also increase accountability, because the openness of the team approach discloses problems and progress in implementation of assignments. They stated, "Our research suggests that teams whose members think in diverse (as opposed to similar) ways and function flexibly across a variety of task types (rather than focusing just on one) are likely to be associated with effective leadership" (p. 8-9).

Their observation is consistent with the large number of responses in our study that referred to appointing or restructuring the senior management team as the most effective strategy in turning around the institution. A third of the presidents in our survey indicated they had appointed new members and/or restructured the senior management team. These salvaging presidents did not expect to turn things around by themselves, but rather as team leaders.

Robert Knott brought in team members he already knew when he went to Tusculum College. There were four, including Knott, who came from other institutions where he had worked with them; they didn't have to spend time learning each other and how each reacted. He opined that this was important to note this "...because you know how difficult it is to bring in new people, adjust, and get expectations together."

Thomas deWitt developed a team of senior administrators to share the leadership of Lasell College. He said that now he makes very few decisions, except the very biggest, and that he had had almost no turnover in twelve years in the entire senior staff except one for illness and one termination. The reason, he believes is that he has empowered them. When he goes on the road for three or four weeks, he doesn't call in because he feels confidence in his team and that if there is a crisis, they will handle it. He also does not believe in micromanaging his team - he takes on his projects, and they do the job of managing the place. The team meets every other week or so to discuss issues and make collective decisions. He says there are no individual decisions.

Another key element in organizational development for the presidents in the study was meeting regularly and consulting with faculty. Several of the presidents who were interviewed sought to actively engage and support the faculty. Robert Knott began by inviting the full-time faculty to his house twice a month, to meet on the side porch and discuss the Tusculum College mission statement along with reading and discussing historical Tusculum documents and even some Cicero, whose villa is the source of Tusculum's name. This was followed by curriculum development. Knott recalled that under the previous administration, the faculty had not really felt that they had the latitude to take ownership of the program and curriculum. What he did was to get them started, get out of their way, and let them develop some pride of ownership. This strategy was also noted by Leslie and Fretwell (1996) in their study of Tusculum College, one of the thirteen encompassed in their research

At United States International University, Garry Hays found many good faculty members who had suffered for many years and were "beaten down" by the situation at the University. Hays said that what happened was that most of the faculty would teach their classes but had otherwise withdrawn from the University. So one of his challenges very early on was to get the faculty involved again, more than just teaching their classes. He said that they worked pretty hard on that and still do. For example, there had been no faculty senate until Hays' interim predecessor started one and developed with the faculty a constitution for shared governance.

When Neil Hoffman returned to Otis College of Art and Design, he sat and listened at the faculty planning meetings while the faculty discussed how to organize the faculty into a governance structure. Hoffman recalled that, "At one point, someone said, 'Neil will tell us what to do.' Someone said, 'But he's the boss.' He didn't rise to the bait and said, 'I believe that this has to be created by you.'" He told them about five schools that had good models, and the faculty ended up with one of them. "However, when it was done, it was their investment," said Hoffman.

Lesson #6: Leadership Makes a Difference at a Struggling Institution

Thirty-three of the thirty-six presidents in our study reported that their leadership and communication skills played most heavily in salvaging their institution. Each of the presidents interviewed in depth provided vivid examples of the dramatic steps they had to take as leaders to turn their institutions around. Thomas deWitt led the transformation of Lasell College from a two-year to a four-year institution, and then from a women's college to a co-ed institution; the latter also occurred under the leadership of Peggy Stock at Colby-Sawyer College. One president convinced the insurers of the burned residence to allow her to use the funds to initiate a major refurbishing of the campus. Alan Guskin took control of Antioch University, enforcing tough budget rules and imposing a plan that would ensure survival. Stephen Morgan appointed a trustee-faculty-staff committee to increase revenues and control expenditures and then implemented its advice at the University of LaVerne. Neil Hoffman launched a long-range planning process that included community leaders, who joined with the campus leadership in defining the mission and vision of Otis College of Art and Design. Donald Averill tackled accreditation issues head-on at Palo Verde College and resorted to "canal diplomacy" to hash out faculty-related problems that had festered too long. Jerry Lee closed schools and let go dozens of administrators at National University. Garry Hays closed programs, consolidated schools, cut the payroll, and created a new non-profit corporation that bought the campus and leased it back to United States International University, giving it enough money to pay off the secured creditors. Robert Knott put together a five-year financial plan in only two weeks, in order to get bank financing to keep the doors open at Tusculum College.

As noted above in Lesson #2, Birnbaum (1992) described two types of presidential leadership at colleges and universities: instrumental and interpretive. According to Birnbaum, exemplary presidents exercise both types of leadership, and "...offer the possibility that while presidential leadership may have only a marginal effect on institutions most of the time, it potentially may have a major effect in renewing institutional values and improving organizational performance under certain conditions" (p. 167).

Those certain conditions surely apply to institutions *in extremis*. It could be argued that the presidents in our study began as instrumental leaders and then became interpretative leaders as well. The actions they took immediately were instrumental - holding meetings with constituencies, reorganizing the administration, cutting budgets, hiring consultants, and freezing expenditures. But the most effective strategies for turning around their institutions were both instrumental and interpretive - general organizational development, fiscal planning, enrollment management, public relations, changing board membership and functioning, strategic planning, fundraising, redefining or re-enforcing the mission, and developing new academic programs.

The skills that the salvaging presidents felt made the most difference in salvaging the institution were interpretive skills - leadership, communication, organizational management, strategic planning, interpersonal, and public relations. In Birnbaum's (1992) words, these interpretive skills made it possible for the presidents to save their institutions by "altering perceptions of institutional functioning and the relationship of the institution to its environment" (p. 154).

Alan Guskin described how his leadership style changed as the crisis abated at Antioch University. The hardest thing for him to understand was how it was possible to be a strong leader, which he admits he was in the first two years, in an inherently collaborative institution. In questioning how an institution that is so egalitarian would permit somebody to be a tough, high-profile leader, he concluded that everybody knew that if the systems weren't built, controls weren't in place, and that there wasn't somebody giving them some hope and a sense of direction, the place was not going to make it. So they gave him that freedom, but once things were getting healthy, he went back to a more collaborative, collegial decision-making style, which was more his natural style.

For Stephen Morgan, of the University of La Verne, leadership is incremental, and mostly common sense. He noted that he had learned that institutions take sequential steps; very seldom do they take quantum leaps from point A to point D without going through B and C. In his experience, the steps have to be sequential, building on what was done before. As he looked back over fourteen years, he could see that the institution had made enormous progress, but that it had been one step at a time. He believes that a lot of it is common sense and finds it amazing, as he looks at other institutions, how frequently top leadership isn't leading with common sense.

As Leslie and Fretwell (1996) concluded in their study of thirteen struggling institutions, and as demonstrated in our study, leaders "...need patience, sensitivity, and communication skills far beyond what they might need in a hierarchical setting of command and control" (p. 237). They also noted that the biggest mistake leaders can make in a crisis is to confuse patience with passivity. "Passivity in the face of a crisis can be fatal to the organization" (p. 237) Certainly, the presidents in our study were not passive.

Whatever the leadership style, the presidents in our study demonstrated that leadership - characterized by their integrity, competence, vision, and ability to inspire, characteristics cited by people across cultures, professions, and economic conditions (Coffey 2007) - makes a significant difference at struggling institutions.

In his singularly insightful exploration of the role of leadership in higher education, Bogue (2007) indicates that successful leaders are those who work, knowingly or unknowingly, with operative theories of role, task, and effectiveness. They leave their institutions with a leadership legacy "...of faculty and staff talents of greater promise, worthy goals achieved in concert with faculty and staff, organizations honoring and enhancing those talents, and value cultures that inspire others with curiosity, courage, and compassion" (p. xii). The salvaging presidents in our study have decidedly provided their institutions with such leadership legacies.

Lesson #7: A Salvaging President May Not Have a Traditional Academic Background

The salvaging presidents in our study saw things differently, and did things differently, than their predecessors. For as many as a third of the presidents, their ability to see and do things differently may have been the result of their non-traditional backgrounds.

Of the 2,105 presidents surveyed in a profile of American college presidents (Greene 1988), only 6.5 percent came from outside academe. A total of 59 percent of these presidents served as presidents or vice presidents of colleges or universities just prior to assuming their position. Mobility among types of institutions was limited. The data showed that 32 percent of the presidents were internal candidates, and another 36 percent came from the same type of institution as the one they were selected to serve. Thus, 68 percent came from the same or a similar institution.

The backgrounds and limited mobility of presidents surveyed by Green (1988) are consistent with the work of Greenwood and Ross (1996) who noted that presidential search committees commonly use two yardsticks in measuring candidates: "[F]irst, how close in complexity the candidate's current budget, personnel, and programmatic responsibilities are to the responsibilities of the position under consideration; and second, the academic stature the candidate would bring to the institution..." (P. 24)

They further pointed out that the typical path to a presidency includes background as a full professor with tenure in a prestigious research university; publications in refereed journals; presentations at international scholarly conferences; demonstrated ability to develop revenue through grants, student recruitment and retention, donations, and state support; service as an academic department head, dean, and vice president; and demonstrated vision, leadership, and skill in management, finance, and planning. The exception, Greenwood and Ross noted, is that institutions with special challenges may search for presidents strong in particular fields such as fundraising, student recruitment and retention, or finance, budget, and administration.

Although the presidents in our survey most often mentioned depth and breadth of experience in senior administration, planning, finance, public relations, fundraising, and accreditation, Greenwood's and Ross' first yardstick, similarities in the candidate's current responsibilities with the new job was mentioned by only 20 percent of them. Seven indicated they had experience salvaging another institution, and two mentioned they had experience with a similar institution.

Greenwood's and Ross' second yardstick - academic stature - was mentioned by only a third of the presidents in our survey, although eleven said their background as a scholar and leader of faculty was a reason for their selection. Further, a third of the presidents did not have traditional academic backgrounds, were chosen more for their non-academic skills than their professional stature, and used mostly non-academic strategies to turn their institutions around.

One of our interviewed participants did not follow the more or less traditional academic progression from Instructor to Provost in a discipline; rather, hers was exclusively in student affairs. She is convinced she wouldn't have survived the first year, dealing with the trauma of residential fires, a substantial deficit, and waning enrollments had she not had strong crisis management experience.

Garry Hays thinks his corporate experience was one of the factors that was appealing to the Board of United States International University. They liked that combination, and to him personally it was invaluable. He recognized that his was an educational institution and therefore could not be run exactly like a corporation, but he also recognized that it must be bottom-line oriented. In his view, if an institution doesn't have strong management, it's not going to make it. Hays also thinks the other way his corporate experience helped was in dealing with the business community in the San Diego area. As the business people got to know him and became aware of his background, he was not viewed just as an academic type and that enabled him to become significantly involved with groups like the Chamber of Commerce where people knew that he had been in business and could look at him as one of them.

The presidents in our survey therefore believed they were selected because they were strong in particular fields - administration, planning, finance, public relations, fundraising, and accreditation. This places them among the exceptions cited by Greenwood and Ross, namely those appointed because of specific strengths. Being chosen for particular strengths or skills may be an advantage for the salvaging president.

In commenting on his research with Hungerford (cited above), Alan Hamlin (1990) said, "[T]he duties of many private (and public) college presidents will require greater communication and marketing skills than in the past. The ultimate success or failure of a college in overcoming a financial crisis will depend in large measure on the vision, enthusiasm, and marketing skills of its leader" (p. 13-14)

These three factors cited by Hamlin - vision, enthusiasm, and marketing skills - were mentioned by the presidents in our survey as important factors in their ability to turn around their institutions. These are not traditional academic skills, and many of the presidents in our study who used these skills did not have traditional academic backgrounds.

More on Lesson # 7 from the Literature

Hahn (1995) argued that universities long for the ideal president, someone of mythic proportions, a hero on a charger who can sweep down and solve intractable problems with dazzling strokes of invention. The problem, Hahn said, is that the standards of success are so unreasonable that no president can measure up to them. As a result, "...failure is endemic in the ranks of presidents" (p. 13). An inability to balance the paradoxical demands of leadership - being visionary and a steward, active and reflective, consistent and creative - causes many presidents to fail according to Alan Guskin and Mary Marcy (Guskin and Marcy 2002).

McLaughlin (1996) noted that presidents are expected to take on an extraordinarily broad range of responsibilities: "The all-encompassing scope of presidential responsibilities means that even someone with considerable strengths in some areas will be less proficient in others. The President may be judged inadequate for the job, when in fact the job is virtually un-doable" (p.16). By contrast, she noted that a president chosen because of particular skills or strengths needed to salvage an institution will be judged by how well he or she uses those skills or strengths to resolve the crisis at hand. The range of constituent expectations may therefore be focused on the president's strengths. Areas in which the president has fewer skills or strengths may be accepted as less important areas during the time of crisis.

A pertinent example of McLaughlin's scenario occurred with the April 2001 appointment of Edwin I. Colodny, a former chief executive officer of US Airways with virtually no experience in academe, as Interim President of the University of Vermont. In his 13-month stint, he got the board to take on a debt to build much-needed student housing, worked with students to undermine an annual gathering of marijuana smokers, eliminated the dental-hygiene program by transferring it to the Vermont State Colleges for some $500,000 to $750,000, made cuts in continuing education saving some $1 million, dropped five of twenty-seven intercollegiate sports saving about $50,000, and helped secure a donation for a research center. To show its appreciation for all this, the Vermont legislature gave the University more money than it had requested!

In their provocative essay, Atwell and Wilson (2003) noted, "If college and university presidents continue to be drawn from the ranks of persons who are primarily scholars, there will be an increasing disconnection between the skills necessary to lead our institutions and the qualifications of their leaders" (p. 24). They urged that institutions looking to the future should seek leaders with demonstrated skills honed within large non-profit organizations, governments, or corporations. Among current presidents with non-traditional backgrounds, they cited: David Boren, a former governor and U. S. Senator, as President of the University of Oklahoma; Peter McPherson, formerly in banking and federal government, as President of

Michigan State University; Robert King, formerly in major state government positions, as Chancellor of the State University of New York; and Donna Shalala, following eight years as U. S. Secretary of Health and Human Services, as President of the University of Miami. And recall that General Dwight ("Ike") Eisenhower was President of Columbia University! It was rumored at the time that the faculty believed they were getting his brother, Milton, the well-known economist.

Added to this list are: software executive Lee T. Todd, Jr. as President of the University of Kentucky; former U. S. Senator Bob Kerry as President of New School University; former U. S. Ambassador Richard F. Celeste, as President of Colorado College; and former U. S. Treasurer Lawrence Summers, as President, recently resigned, of Harvard University (Basinger 2002). Basinger also cites an American Council on Education study, based on a 2001 survey, that the percentage of leaders whose immediate prior positions were outside higher education rose from 6 percent in 1998 to 12 percent in 2001. Further, if specialized institutions such as business and chiropractic schools are included, the percentage of presidents with non-academic backgrounds rose from nearly 8 percent in 1998 to nearly 15 percent in 2001.

This changing landscape of university and college presidential searches has been succinctly described in two companion articles by representatives of very well-known and widely experienced executive search firms, R. William Funk, of Korn/Ferry International, and Theodore J. Marchese, of Academic Search Consultation Service. Funk (2006) notes that, "The time when boards sought a genial, well-liked and long-tenured 'Mr. Chips' has passed" (p. 20). Instead, he asserts that in addition to the usual set of skills, boards seek different leadership models and skills, especially a proven ability to raise large sums of money, that are often cultivated outside the walls of academe. Marchese (2006) also underscores that the emphasis on fundraising "...keeps pushing to the top" (p. 22). He also cites an American Council on Education comparison of presidents appointed in 2002 with those in 1986 that showed more of the recent appointees to be in a second presidency (20 percent) or from outside higher education (15 percent) and to be five years older than the earlier presidents (57.5 vs. 52.3 years of age), which he attributes to "...proof of fund-raising ability" (p.22).

The statistics quoted by Marchese are from a study conducted by the American Council on Education (June 2007), which also notes that the percentage of presidents who were age 61 and older in 1986 and 2006 were respectively 13.9 and 49.3! However, contrary to the previous declaration about more presidents coming from outside academe, the percentages of those serving as provost before becoming president in 1986 and 2006 had actually increased from 22.5 to 31.4

Conclusion

In conclusion, it is a given that the turf of contemporary higher education institutions continues to change because of demographic, economic, social, and global factors, amongst others. Would our salvaging presidents be successful in meeting these new and continuing challenges along with the specifics of an *in extremis* institution? We believe they would and could. They proved they could do so in the institutions they salvaged. Given their instrumental and interpretative leadership skills, their adroit uses of structural, human resources, political, and symbolic reframing strategies separately and in various combinations, their dogged determination to be successful in whatever they undertook, their courage - even audacity - to face the challenge, and their profound personal and professional integrity, these presidents exemplify strikingly the qualities evidenced in a salvaging president.

Appendix A

The Survey Instrument and Responses

To save space, the blank portions that provided for comments have been deleted; these comments are direct quotations with citations where permitted. The presidents and their institutions, where permitted, are found in the Acknowledgment section.

SURVEY OF PRESIDENTS WHO HAVE SALVAGED INSTITUTIONS

Please return to:

Dr. Edward J. Kormondy
1388 Lucile Avenue
Los Angeles, CA 90026

Respondent's name:

Institution described in this survey:

I. The Situation at the Institution as You Found It

1. The major institutional *in extremis* issues which I had to address were (check all that apply):

    _27_ financial exigency
    _23_ seriously flagging new enrollments
    _24_ high rate of student turnover (dropouts, failures, etc.)
    _29_ very small endowment
    _15_ decline in gifts and donations
    _31_ lack of institutional and program planning
    _13_ poor quality academic programs
    _17_ outdated or declining academic programs
    _22_ poor quality student services and student facilities
    _3_ crime on campus
    _13_ significant increase in competition
    _27_ inadequate fundraising

  __23_ conflict between administration and faculty
  __8_ vote of no confidence in the president by the faculty
  __27_ negative public image of the institution
  __13_ high turnover of senior administrative personnel
  __23_ conflict between administration and faculty
  __8_ vote of no confidence in the president by the faculty
  __10_ administration preempting the role of faculty in academic
       governance
  __10_ improperly constituted Board (trustees, directors, regents, etc.)
  __10_ micromanagement by Board and/or external entities (e.g.,
       legislature)
  __13_ lack of support by Board members
  __20_ potential loss of accreditation owing to one or more of the above or
       other factors
  _____ other (please identify briefly)

Administration
* Presidential turnover
* Mismanagement by previous administration
* Outdated institutional research and financial systems
* Lack of operational policies (Thomas Stauffer)

Academics
* Loss of institutional focus particularly in specialized area, e.g., education
* Poor administrative systems (Paul LeBlanc)

Financial
* Demographics, economy, etc. resulted in three years of increasing
deficits - the college was technically bankrupt
* Continuing deficits
* Failure to pay state and federal taxes and no audited financial statements
* Inadequate financial and management systems
* Selling of assets - land
* No fundraising; no budgeting system (Thomas Stauffer)
* Defalcation (Richard Cox)

Institutional Climate
* Poor self image
* Community morale after a "very public" retrenchment
* Resistance to change within the university (culture of the organization)
(Kent Keith)

Faculty
* Faculty union and faculty senate in conflict
* Institution placed on AAUP "List of Censured Institutions" before I came
* Some faculty with false credentials; no governance (Thomas Stauffer)

Governing Board
* One board member faces a recall election
* A good but aging Board suffering from "Board Fatigue" (Paul LeBlanc)
* Outdated Bylaws (Thomas Stauffer)

Physical Plant
* Physical plant in much need of attention (Paul LeBlanc)
* Massive deferred maintenance (Francis Hazard)

Public Relations
* Public relations minimal (Francis Hazard)

Athletics
* Athletic compliance infractions
* 50% in athletic team enrollments

Other
* Legal problems
* Church denomination in decline; 50% of enrollment incarcerated (Francis Hazard)
* No technology (Thomas Stauffer)
* Theft (Richard Cox)

Please describe (briefly or extensively) the specifics of the situation if the above descripter(s) is not sufficient.

Accreditation
* College was placed on probation prior to arrival for planning, program review, catalog, micromanagement by board, and financial concerns (Donald Averill)
* The regional accrediting association to action to de-accredit the institution.
* Accrediting association put university on warning two months before I started as president, there were forty issues of concern in the report that we needed to address to save accreditation (Kent Keith)
* The precipitating incident was a verdict of "show cause" from the accrediting association, the Board took over at this point. The student

body was 80% foreign, and there were not adequate programs in place either to give these students the American education that they had a right to expect, or to recruit American students.

* Two weeks prior to my formal appointment, the institution was placed on probation by NCA [North Central Association of Schools and Colleges]. The institution had gone through a foiled merger attempt with a sister university advocated/led by the previous president.

Finances

* There was the sense that the institution was spinning out of control and that, in fact, the institution was financially in danger of closing in eight-twelve months (Alan Guskin)
* Institution had ten years of one-year presidents, then my predecessor stayed six years but failed to deal with finances and doubled debt to 4 million during his tenure, a key classroom building (science/math) had been condemned, and no plans were in place to replace it. salaries were so low that staff turnover and quality was a problem (Francis Hazard)
* Board was entertaining proposals for sale, banks refused to lend money, and loss of D&O insurance (Richard Wylie)
* College had been very successful for many years, but demographics, economy, etc. had resulted in three years of increasing operating deficits - the college was technically bankrupt.

Board

* There was a power struggle between the Board majority (four), which is union supported and based at the larger of the two colleges, and the Board minority (three), which supports the senate and is based in the smaller, newer campus
* A good but aging Board suffering from "Board Fatigue," physical plant in much need of attention, and poor administrative systems (Paul LeBlanc)

Other

* President fired seven faculty before he left, lots of unfilled promises, no dramatic vision (just tinkering) to transform the institution (Thomas de Witt)
* Racial incident on campus generated statewide and national publicity, all of it negative (Michael Bassis)
* Previous president had been removed by the Board, but a one-year interim president had served very well
* In the preceding three years, a planning committee of Board members, administration and faculty had recommended consolidation of all programs on the ... campus, conflict erupted, and administration was

stone-walled from implementing this

* College was undergoing a contentious separation form a middle/high school and establishing its own Board of Trustees (James Waddell)

* Five of eight senior positions , including that of the president, were in acting status owing to resignations or terminations over a six-month period (Edward Kormondy)

* Outdated Bylaws, lack of operational policies, no fund-raising, some faculty with false credentials, no governance, no budgeting systems, no technology (Thomas Stauffer)

2. Which of the above situations or issues were known to you at the time you accepted your appointment, and which surfaced within the first month or two after your appointment/arrival?

    a. Known to me when I accepted appointment:

    b. Surfaced during the first month or two after my appointment/arrival:

(Note: these responses are discussed in Part Four)

II. Reasons for Your Appointment as President

3. What in your experience and/or background led to you being selected as the person to "salvage" the institution (check all that apply):

    __31__ depth and breadth of senior administrative experience
    __11__ background as a scholar and leader of faculty
    __18__ financial experience
    __24__ planning experience
    __8__ campus/physical plant experience
    __14__ fundraising experience
    __15__ public relations experience
    __13__ accreditation experience
        __8__ member (past or present) of an accrediting body
        __11__ member/chair of visiting accreditation teams
    __7__ previous salvaging of another institution
    __5__ ready availability (e.g., in retirement, between positions)
    __9__ previous relationship with the institution
    __7__ previous personal or professional relationship with Board member(s)
    _____ other (please identify briefly)

Turnaround Experience

* Worked in another urban, politically troubled institution
    * Reputation as a turnaround specialist (Neil Hoffman)
    * Five years of turnaround experience as Executive Vice President as another institution (Michael Bassis)
    * Turned around Lasell's # 1 competitor in 3 years (Thomas de Witt)
    * Reputation as a turnaround specialist

Administrative Experience
* Human resources
* Seven months as interim president
* Working with unions
* Ten successful years as chancellor of a public university (Alan Guskin)
* Familiarity with system's policies, budget and faculty concerns
* International, continuing education, and alternative delivery systems
* Managing complex budgets
* Prior to coming to _____ I served as V.P. for Continuing and External Education at ____ - developed several offsite campuses (two in Europe, one in Los Angeles); resuscitated and redirected a large performing arts division to viability; negotiated two successive contracts with unionized faculty; expanded programming and modes of delivery for continuing education and fostered relationships with several international institutions and organizations (Laurence Conner)

Non-Academic Experience
* A combination of successful experience as a CEO in higher education and for ten years in the corporate world (Garry Hays)
* Faculty liked my academic background while board liked my entrepreneurial and corporate experience and sensibility (Paul LeBlanc)
* Entrepreneurial and business background (Richard Wylie)
* Previous experience as a mayor and on economic development boards

Personal Qualities/Characteristics
* Passion for the institution
* Energy and creativity - courage
* Open, direct style of management and board-based consulting practice
* Institution was attracted because of my resignation from a previous nine-year presidency when head of system refused to support a personnel decision (Thomas Stauffer)

Desperation
* Problems so severe, no one would want the position (Chatt Wright)
* Difficulty in attracting candidates - I was the lessor of two or three evils (Stephen Morgan)

* Management style as evidenced in a similar kind of institution
* Board was unable to find anybody they felt was qualified and also willing to take the job
* I was asked to take the job, even though I had not applied for it (Kent Keith

Please describe (briefly or extensively) the specifics of your pertinent experience.

(Note: These responses are discussed in Part Four)

III. Your short-Term Actions and Long-Term Strategies

4. What actions did you take more or less immediately (i.e., during the first month or two) to address the situation at hand (check all that apply)?

    __35_ in depth meetings with
    > __33_ Board
    > __35_ faculty
    > __33_ staff
    > > __5_ administrative only
    > > __17_ all staff
    > __15_ students
    > __12_ alumni leadership
    > __9_ major donors and/or sponsoring organizations
    > __12_ local media
    > __18_ accrediting body(ies)
    > __15_ community leaders
    > __6_ other constituency(ies) (please briefly indicate the group(s))
    > Vendors and lenders; banking community (4 banks) and industrial/business leaders; legal, athletics, church; national associations and regional media; all school superintendents of 13 local school districts; numerous civic organizations
    __10_ freeze all expenditures
    __18_ cut the budget
    __25_ reorganized the administration
    __16_ retained consultants on specific major issues
    _____ other (please briefly indicate)

Planning
* Completed "future search" planning model to bring constituents and stakeholders together (Donald Averill)
* Started planning process for the rest of the year and listened a lot

* Held workshops with faculty, staff, and Regents to develop three-year plan to respond to WASC accreditation report (Kent Keith)
* Focused on mission by redefining it followed by development of a strategic plan
* Involved everyone immediately in long-range planning (Neil Hoffman)

Management
* Launched several high visibility projects
*Took an operations management approach, hired most faculty to get their support, immediately set a vision, and started work on 1) changing the name to delete Junior and 2) plan to make it a 4-year institution (Thomas de Witt)
* Took charge of an institution spinning out of control (Alan Guskin)
* Constituted a broad-based collaborative response team to legal and athletic problems
* Public-relations campaign, constructed new residence hall, and initiated three BS degrees (Richard Wylie)

Budget
* Pushed productivity and innovation and reprioritized budget
* Renegotiated contracts with external bodies, released consultants, and negotiated credit for three-year period (Robert Knott)

Personnel
* Terminated eight or nine VPs, several deans, and a number of staff (Garry Hays)
* Wrote basic Bylaws and policies, outsourced IT, and fired people (Thomas Stauffer)
* Dismissed VP, established new admissions, student aid and registrar offices, and began to contact alumni
* Fired eight people
* Appointing an expert CFO
* Froze hiring of full-time faculty and creation of new positions
* Closed satellite campus (Richard Cox)

Consultation
* Two-day retreat with all constituencies to discuss challenges facing the college (Paul Le Blanc)
* Intensive legal consultation on accreditation and finances and telephone communication with all students

Academic Programs
* Asked faculty to develop a new academic vision for the college (Michael

Bassis)

5.   What long-term or longer-term strategy(ies) was developed in the first few
weeks/months (check all that apply)?

     __32_ instituted long-range/strategic planning
     __18_ redefined the institution's mission
     __16_ developed market niches in order to compete more effectively for
           students
     __29_ instituted new student recruitment programs
     __21_ instituted new student retention programs
     __10_ changed admissions standards (either more or less stringent)
     __21_ instituted a fundraising campaign
     __19_ instituted a public relations campaign
     ___8_ increased tuition
     __13_ increased financial aid
     __29_ improved relationships between the administration and faculty
     __20_ upgraded or added academic programs
     __16_ eliminated some academic programs
     __16_ upgraded student services and student facilities
     __22_ upgraded campus/physical plant
     __17_ eliminated positions
     __15_ created new positions
     ___3_ reduced crime on campus
     __11_ outsourced some operations (e.g., bookstore, cafeteria)
     __20_ reconstituted the Board
     __30_ trained the Board in regard to its role
     _____ other (please briefly indicate)

* We did almost all of the things on our action plan over three years,
moving in nearly all directions at once to save accreditation (Kent Keith)
* Signs of enrollment declines had only begun to be revealed at the onset
of my role as president. Within the first semester, attrition accelerated and
recruitment began to flag. With a limited reserve, no ability to borrow
against its assets and an image challenge while on probation, I began the
first downsizing phase. As conditions worsened (even after the sanction of
probation was removed), a more carefully planned but quickly executed
"right sizing" phase II began. Every aspect of the University was, at some
level, modified. For cxample, the academic structure was altered from 7
academic divisions housing 15 departments offering 32 majors, to 6
departments offering 12 majors. (Laurence Conner)
* District-wide organization development effort based on corporate values
* Developed sense of hope, rebuilt board (Alan Guskin)

* Listened more, focused on church relations/societal needs
* Bond refinancing (Jerry Lee)
* Conducted two-year audit review in two months and carefully managed cash resources
* Commitment to balanced budget, enrollment growth, and faculty support (Thomas de Witt)
* Fired dean of students and athletic coach (Michael Bassis)
* Established national honor societies where none existed (Francis Hazard)
* Comprehensive enrollment management introduced
* Visible signage
* New residence hall and new international programs (Richard Wylie)
* Had an action list of 123 items and completed all (Thomas Stauffer)
* Crime problem in student records corrected
* New academic programs
* Planning process for following year and five years beyond
* Began legal process to deal with previous administration's lawsuit (Richard Cox)

IV. The Turnaround

6. How long did it take to "turn around" the situation(s)?

        0 less than a year
       11 one to two years
       17 two to five years
        2 more than five years
        8 still in process after _2_ months or _3 - 4_ years

7. Which actions or strategies were most effective in turning around the situation? Please indicate the three or four that made the most difference:

        42 general organizational development
        19 fiscal planning
        13 enrollment management
        11 public relations
        10 board membership
        10 strategic planning
         9 development
         6 mission and vision
         6 academic programs

8. What particular aspects of your personality/experience/background played most heavily in "salvaging" the institution (check all that apply)?

    __33__ leadership skills
    __28__ organizational management
    __27__ strategic planning skills
    __16__ personnel management
    __17__ professional stature/reputation
    __27__ interpersonal skills
    __33__ communication skills
    __16__ academic expertise
    __17__ accreditation knowledge
    __17__ fiscal acumen
    __15__ fundraising skills
    __27__ public relation skills
    _____ other (please describe briefly)

* Energy, entrepreneurial spirit, building an excellent management team, re-energizing faculty (Paul LeBlanc)
* Guts and courage to take on issues and understanding how an organization works
* Alumni relations (Haywood Strickland)
* Persistence, courage, focus, resolve (Michael Bassis)
* Persistence, taking the long view, and not letting day to day adversity get in the way
* Tenacity, perseverance, optimism (Kent Keith)
* An honest, reasonably bright, hard-working person who let it be known that every decision was in the best interest of the institution
* Luck, family (Jerry Lee)
* Especially oral communication, selecting good people, bull headedness
* Longevity and credibility with the institution (Richard Cox)
* Just doing it, being action oriented (Thomas Stauffer)

V. Advice for Presidents

9. What advice would you proffer to presidents selected to salvage an institution?

    __0__ don't do it
    __27__ do it with your eyes wide open
    __4__ do it for a pre-set, agreed-upon term (e.g., four years)
    __9__ make sure that key campus constituencies will support change

_28_ make sure you have Board support

_24_ make sure you have access to all critical information (e.g., budgets, enrollment data)

_15_ make sure you understand the view and requirements of accrediting agencies

_17_ make sure you understand the external forces (e.g., demographic, social, economic, political) that affect the institution

_____ other (please describe briefly)

Personal Attributes

* Be patient and employ several strategies simultaneously
* Don't let your ego become involved, and don't fear failure
* Understand how much energy it takes because success depends on sheer will in some measure (Paul Le Blanc)
* Be committed to the cause and assure yourself it is worthy enough to fail in the attempt and that there is no formula to success
* Make sure you understand and have commitment to believing in others' ideas and the need to manage climate (Neil Hoffman)
* Do it as a labor of love, as a once in a lifetime to make a difference (Michael Bassis)
* Do because you enjoy and become engaged with a challenge, have confidence in being a risk-taker, and have several key supporters (Richard Wylie)
* Make sure you have the physical stamina to confront many challenges simultaneously because you must be a skilled multi-task manager
* Enjoy it - it is a challenge that has special rewards
* I outworked everybody and resistance faded away (Thomas Stauffer)
* Be willing to use bold, creative approaches outside of the usual way of doing business in the academic setting
* Be patient (Daniel Ritchie)
* Take the long view and do not be afraid to move slowly to get support for major shifts in the culture

Planning/Management

* Have an independent financial audit done beforehand to assure issues are approved from a fiscal perspective
* Do an environmental scan to see if the college has the potential to survive (Donald Averill)
* Develop a clear set of "turnaround" goals or initiatives (Jerry Lee)
* Try to find out in advance what various constituencies expect of you (Francis Hazard)
* Try to salvage the institution by build on the values of the culture since organizational cultures tend to resist change (Kent Keith)

Personnel
* Bring in (or find within the institution) good people to help and whom you can trust - don't do it if you are not committed and willing to spend enormous amounts of time and energy nor if you cannot handle stress - and be willing to employ bold creative approaches outside the ususal way of doing business in the academic setting (Garry Hays)
* Select and appoint competent/passionate people
* Make sure you have a team that is committed to the same plan and committed to the long haul (Richard Cox)

Contractual
* Make sure you have a good contract for at least 3 years and only do it if you have been a successful president because you can't learn the needed skills on the job (Alan Guskin)
* A fixed period for the president during the turnaround may be advisable (Laurence Conner)

10.   If this survey omitted any aspect of your salvaging experience that you believe should have been included, please indicate:

* The tremendous need to have a support structure and a senior team that is extremely capable because you can't do it alone
* Be ready for surprises and loss of ground (Donald Averill)
* Timing is important - make sure you have options if you fail, that is know your line of retreat
* One runs into levels of how much change fan be tolerated how fast across constituencies (Paul LeBlanc)
* The passion and commitment to the values and legacy of the institution give a sense of purpose to deal with the difficulty issues (and craziness) and sustenance when there are new problems or things are not going as well as you like (Alan Guskin)
* Set the design criteria for change and empower faculty and others to develop ownership (Michael Bassis)
* There is an emotional cost I did not anticipate that cannot be shared with those who support you, that is knowing you are associated with an institution that is less than most of its neighbors and comparables - your desire to succeed must overcome (Francis Hazard)
* Create a climate of trust and shared vision (James Waddell)
* Confidence in the power of change and belief in one's ability to persuade and channel opinions (Richard Wylie)
* The institution needed to regain its own pride and confidence
* Personal aspects of energy, confidence, good health, sense of humor, and willingness to take on a project are the most important, and also not

caring if anybody got in the way (Thomas Stauffer)
* There are certain personality traits (*e.g.*, competitiveness) that find salvaging an institution very attractive and personally satisfying (Jerry Lee)
* One cannot overemphasize the importance of the Board

11.   You have my permission to use (check those that apply):

       _____ my name _____ the institution's name _____ neither

_____ _____
(Signature)   (Date)

Thank you sincerely for your assistance in this project

Appendix B

About the Authors

Edward J. Kormondy

Edward J. Kormondy received a BA *(Summa cum laude)* in Biology from Tusculum College (1950) and a MS (1951) and PhD (1955) in Zoology from the University of Michigan.

From 1955-57 he served as Instructor in Zoology and Curator of Insects, Museum of Zoology, University of Michigan, as Assistant Professor to Professor of Biology at Oberlin College (1957-68), and Faculty Member, The Evergreen State College, 1971-79. Administrative appointments included: Director, Commission on Undergraduate Education in the Biological Sciences (1968-71); Dean of Natural Sciences (1972-73) and Provost (1973-78), The Evergreen State College; Provost of the University of Southern Maine (1979-82); Vice President for Academic Affairs, California State University-Los Angeles (1982-86); Chancellor, University of Hawai'i-Hilo/West Oahu (1986-93); President, University of West Los Angeles (1995-97); Special Assistant to the President, Pacific Oaks College and Children's School (2000-05); and Acting President, Tusculum College (Summer 2007).

Kormondy has published more than 60 research articles in ecology, environmental science, biology, biomedical and ecological ethics, science education, and most recently, on minority education in China. He is the author or co-author of eight books (e.g., *Concepts of Ecology,* 4th edition, 1995 and *Fundamentals of Human Ecology* 1998) and edited or co-edited eight anthologies in ecology and biology. In addition to extensive college and high-school level

consulting on administration and biology/ecology curricula, he has served on numerous accrediting teams for the Northeast and Northwest regional accrediting associations as well as for both colleges and schools for the Western Association of Schools and Colleges on whose senior and schools commissions he served. He currently serves as Chair of the Board of Trustees of the University of West Los

Angeles and as Vice Chair of the Board of Trustees of Tusculum College.

He has been recognized by *Who's Who in America* as well as several international *"Who's Who,"* received an honorary Doctor of Science from Tusculum College in 1997, and was awarded the title of Chancellor Emeritus, University of Hawai'i-Hilo in 2000. He is a member of Sigma Xi, a Fellow of the American Association for the Advancement of Science, Past President of the National Association of Biology Teachers, and Past Secretary of the Ecological Society of America.

Kormondy's address is: 1388 Lucile Avenue, Los Angeles, CA 90026-1520.

Kent M. Keith

Kent M. Keith received a BA (1970) from Harvard University, a MA (1977) from Oxford University, a JD (1977) from the University of Hawai'i, and a EdD (1996) from the University of Southern California.

His period of private law practice (1977-79) was followed by service in the State of Hawai'i (1979-86), the last three years as Director Planning and Economic Development and work in the private enterprise (1986-89), the last two as Vice President for Public Relations and Business Development, Castle and Cooke Properties. He served as President of Chaminade University of Honolulu from 1989-95 from which he resigned to purse a EdD. From 1998-2004, he served as Senior Vice President for Development and Communication for the Honolulu YMCA. He is President of Carlson Keith Corporation and currently serves as the Chief Executive Officer of the Greenleaf Center for Servant-Leadership in Indiana.

Keith has published more than 30 articles of a variety of topics, including higher education. In 2002, *Anyway: The Paradoxical Commandments* was published by G. P. Putnam's Sons. He served on the Executive Committee of the Western Association of Schools and Colleges (WASC), one of whose then responsibilities was to nominate commissioners for the WASC Commission on Senior Colleges and Universities. He also chaired two WASC accreditation teams that visited colleges in California.

He has been honored by being the first graduate of an Hawai'i public school to be selected as a Rhodes Scholar, one of Ten Outstanding Young Men of American by the United States Jaycees in 1984 (the first so recognized from Hawai'i since 1959), and the Meritorious Dissertation Award from the School of Education, University of Southern California, the highest award given a graduating doctoral student.

Keith's address is: 209 Faulkner Court #206, Carmel, IN 46032.

229

References Cited

Atwell, R. H., and B. C. Wilson. 2003. A nontraditional president may fit just right. *Trusteeship* 11 (2): 24-28.

Basinger, J. 2002. Casting a Wider Net. *Chronicle of Higher Education*. December 13, 2002: A32 - A33.

Bensimon, E. M., and A. Neumann. 1993. *Redesigning Collegiate Leadership: Teams and Teamwork in Higher Education*. Baltimore, MD: Johns Hopkins University.

_____., R. Birnbaum, and A. Neumann. 1989. *Making Sense of Administrative Leadership: The 'L' Word in Higher Education*. Washington, DC: The George Washington University.

Birnbaum, R. 1988. *How Colleges Work: The Cybernetics of Academic Organization and Leadership*. San Francisco: Jossey-Bass Publishers.

_____. 1992. *How Academic Leadership Works: Understanding Success and Failure in the College Presidency*. San Francisco, CA: Jossey Bass Publishers.

Bolman, L. G., and Deal, T. E. 1997. *Reframing Organizations: Artistry, Choice, and Leadership*. Second Edition. San Francisco, CA: Jossey-Bass.

Brodie, H. K. H. and L. Banner. 2005. *The Research University: Presidency in the Late Twentieth Century: A Life Cycle/Case History Approach*. Westport, CT: Praeger Publishers.

Bogue, E. J. 2007. *Leadership Legacy Moments: Vision and Values for Stewards of Collegiate Mission*. Westport, CT.: Praeger Publications.

Burke, J. M. 2003. *2003 Higher Education Directory*. Falls Church, VA: Higher Education Publications, Inc.

_____. 2004. *2004 Higher Education Directory*. Falls Church, VA: Higher Education Publications, Inc.

_____. 2005. *2005 Higher Education Directory*. Falls Church, VA. Higher Education Publications, Inc.

_____. 2006. *2006 Higher Education Directory*. Falls Church, VA. Higher Education Publications, Inc.

_____. 2007. *2007 Higher Education Directory*. Falls Church, VA. Higher Education Publications, Inc.

Carlson, S. 2007. A House Divided. *The Chronicle of Higher Education*, June 29, 2007: A20 - A22.

Clark, B. R.1970. *The Distinctive College: Reed, Antioch, & Swarthmore*. Chicago: Aldine.

Coffey, B. 2007. The Leadership Quotient. *Executive Travel Magazine* May/June 2007: 42-48.

Cohen, M. D., and J. G. March. 1974. *Leadership and Ambiguity: The American College President*. New York: McGraw-Hill Book Co.

Educational Record. Spring/Summer 1996. 77 (2,3).

Fain, P. 2007. Antioch's Closure Signifies the End of an Era. *The Chronicle of Higher Education*, June 22, 2007: A1, A27.

Funk, R. W. 2006. Leadership Fund-Raising and the World Beyond Ivy-Covered Walls. Washington, DC. AASCU's *Public Purpose*, July/August: 20 - 21.

Green, M. F. 1988. *The American College President: A Contemporary Profile.* Washington, DC: American Council on Education.

Greenwood, J. D., and M. Ross. 1996. So you want to be a college president? *Educational Record* 77 (2,3): 24-71.

Guskin, A. E., and M. B. Marcy. 2002. The yin and yang of campus leadership. *Trusteeship.* September/October 2002: 8-12.

Hahn, R. 1995. Getting serious about presidential leadership: Our collective responsibility. *Change* 27 (5): 12-19.

Hamlin, A. 1990. The president as salesman. *The Educational Record* 71 (1): 11-14.

_____., and C. Hungerford. 1988."How private colleges survive a financial crisis: Tools for effective planning and management. *Planning for Higher Education* 17 (2): 29-36.

Heifitz, R. A. 1994. *Leadership without Easy Answers*. Cambridge, MA: The Belknap Press of Harvard University Press.

Ingram, R. T. 1995. *Effective Trusteeship.* Washington, DC: Association of Governing Boards.

June, A. W. 2006. Getting Smarter with Age. *Chronicle of Higher Education,* July 14, 2006: A25 - A27.

_____. 2007. Presidents: Same Look, Different Decade. *The Chronicle of Higher Education*, February 16, 2007: A33-A35.

Keller, G. 2004. *Transforming a College: The Story of a Little-Known College's Strategic Climb to National Distinction.* Baltimore, MD: The Johns Hopkins University Press.

Kerr, C. 1963/1982. *The Uses of the University.* Cambridge, MA: Harvard University Press.

_____. and M. L. Gade. 1986. *The Many Lives of Academic Presidents.* Washington, DC: Association of Governing Boards of Universities and Colleges.

Keyes, R. 2007. Present at the Demise: Antioch College, 1852-2008. *The Chronicle of Higher Education,* July 20, 2007: B8 - B9.

Leslie D. W. and E. K.Fretwell, Jr. 1996. *Wise Moves in Hard Times: Creating and Managing Resilient Colleges and Universities.* San Francisco: Jossey-Bass Publishers.

Marchese, T. J. 2006. The Competition is Fierce. Washington, DC. AASCU's *Public Purpose* July/August: 22-23.

McLaughlin, J. B. 1996. The perilous presidency. *Educational Record* 77 (2,3): 12-17.

Murphy, M. K. (Ed). 1997. *The Advancement President and the Academy.* Phoenix, AZ: American Council on Education and Oryx Press.

Neumann, A., and E. M. Bensimon. 1990. Constructing the presidency: College presidents' images of their leadership roles, a comparative study. *The Journal of Higher Education* 61 (6): 678-701.

Patrick, C., and J. K. Caruthers. Management priorities of college presidents. *Research in Higher Education* 12(3): 195-214.

Powell, J. L. 1995. *Pathways to Leadership: How to Achieve and Sustain Success.* San Francisco: Jossey-Bass Publishers.

Rodenhouse, M. P. 2001. *2001 Higher Education Directory.* Falls Church, VA: Higher Education Publications.

_____. 2002. *2002 Higher Education Directory.* Falls Church, VA: Higher Education Publications.

Rhodes, F. H. T. 2006. After 40 Years of Growth and Change, Higher Education Faces New Challenges. *The Chronicle of Higher Education.* November 24, 2006: A18 - A20.

Rudolph, F. 1962. *The American College and University.* New York: Knopf.

Sellars, J. D. 1994. The warning signs of institutional decline. *Trusteeship* 2 (6): 11-14.

_____. 2005. Lessons learned at the brink. *Trusteeship* 12 (4): 14 - 18.

Tierney, W. G. 1988. *The Web of Leadership: The Presidency in Higher Education.* Greenwich, CT: JAI Press.

van der Werf, M. 2002 Many Colleges May Close or Merge, Standard and Poor's Predicts. *Chronicle of Higher Education,* December 13, 2002: A34.

Zander, A. 1993. *Making Boards Effective. The Dynamics of Nonprofit Governing Boards.* San Francisco, CA: Jossey-Bass Publishers.

Index

236

238